H

David
JULE 2015

mote

mote

the super meeting

The radical way to work together for positive change

David WETHEY

URBANE
Publications

urbanepublications.com

First published in Great Britain in 2015
by Urbane Publications Ltd
Suite 3, Brown Europe House, 33/34 Gleamingwood Drive,
Chatham, Kent ME5 8RZ
Copyright © David Wethey, 2015

A CIP catalogue record for this book is available
from the British Library.

ISBN 978-1-909273-20-7
EPUB 978-1-909273-22-1

Cover design by Julie Martin
Design and Typeset by Julie Martin

Printed in Great Britain by
CPI Group (UK) Ltd, Croydon, CR0 4YY

urbanepublications.com

I dedicate this book to my wife Sue, and my children Matt, Duncs, Bella and Saffy – all of whom believe in my ideas and encourage me to tilt at windmills, despite my inability to make, mend, grow or cook anything.

Also to the hundreds of brilliant colleagues and business friends with whom I have sat for countless hours in unproductive meetings. I can only apologise to you all for not having thought of Mote years ago!

"Can't talk now Dave, I'm in a meeting – with you."

CONTENTS

TESTIMONIALS   9

ACKNOWLEDGEMENTS   12

FOREWORD   15

CHAPTER 1
The joy of meeting   19

CHAPTER 2
Meetings are not all created equal – meet the Super Six!   27

CHAPTER 3
We can't go on meeting like this   43

CHAPTER 4
The damage meetings can do to everyone – and
particularly to our life/work balance   63

CHAPTER 5
People can go wrong in meetings too   85

CHAPTER 6
Time to introduce you to Mote   117

CHAPTER 7
A very little key will open a very heavy door   135

CHAPTER 8
The game plan – getting ready to Mote   169

CHAPTER 9
How to manage a Mote, and run the best meeting ever   191

CHAPTER 10
Ideas into action – the Mote isn't over when it's over   211

CHAPTER 11
Launching Mote into the organisation   219

CHAPTER 12
The secrets of being a great Moter – and a star performer –
at every meeting you attend   247

INSPIRATIONAL WISDOM AND SUGGESTIONS FOR
FURTHER READING   269

TESTIMONIALS

Cilla Snowball CBE, *Group Chairman and Group CEO AMV BBDO, Chair of the Advertising Association*
The essential guide to making meetings productive and purposeful not pointless and painful. A much needed reminder of the constituents of great meetings.

Dame Fiona Woolf CBE, *Former Lord Mayor of London*
I have presided over Motes in the wards of the City of London as Alderman and Lord Mayor – a meeting with its origins in the medieval trading era when collaboration facilitated competition. This book turns the Mote into a modern super meeting, the like of which we have not seen before. Not only does it save one of our scarcest resources, time, but the Spirit of Mote improves the way we work outside the meeting room.

Mike Hughes, *Director General Incorporated Society of British Advertisers (ISBA)*
The 'meeting' is an essential cog in business life, and we tolerate too many bad meetings. Why, and is there a better way? This book addresses the issue head on, suggesting an alternative, innovative approach which promises to transform the event into an experience which is both enjoyable and effective.

Chris Satterthwaite, *CEO Chime Communications*
This is an expert book written by a man whose job it has been to observe successful and unsuccessful meetings. With ways all participants in meetings can make better use of their time and energy I suspect that a 20 per cent improvement in effective meetings in your company will lead to an identical improvement in productivity. That's a book worth reading.

Herve de Clerck, *Founder of Adforum*
This book is about solving the contradictions of our human nature. Productive ideas are the result of building upon each other not fighting against each other. In a new life, David will create a Master in Business Simplification.

Dr Robert Shaw, *Honorary Professor of Marketing Metrics at Cass Business School*
DO NOT READ this book if you love the sound of your own voice, enjoy gossiping all day and can drink endless cups of cold coffee in featureless rooms. If that's not you then embrace David Wethey's antidote to the tedium and traumas of the modern business meeting.

Domonic Lyle, *Director General European Association of Communications Agencies (EACA)*
Having attended often unproductive meetings for the best part of 45 years, it is a matter of regret that this excellent book comes too late to save me from hours of frustration

and boredom. David Wethey has crystallized a dynamic new methodology for managing meetings into a practical guide to a better, results-oriented way of working.

Mote gets my vote.

Jean-Noel Kapferer, *Emeritus Professor of Marketing, HEC Paris*

Today's management mantra commands us to work collaboratively. Hence the multiplication of meetings within companies. But do meetings make people decide? Not really, unless they are designed with that purpose says David Wethey. It is high time this issue was addressed with pragmatism and a clear method. This is the quintessence of MOTE. Most useful.

Harris Diamond, *Chairman & Chief Executive Officer of McCann Worldgroup*

In **Mote**, David Wethey successfully tackles an important business subject that we're all familiar with. He brings his extensive experience to bear in addressing how to make business meetings better. And he also offers keen insights on how meetings themselves can become a more productive component overall in helping organizations to meet their growth goals. This book points the way both to better meetings and better use of meetings.

ACKNOWLEDGEMENTS

My grateful thanks go to all those people who have kindly helped and encouraged me along the way - without you the book could not have been written. I have received a great deal of advice and assistance, but I bear sole responsibility for the book's contents.

Sarah Todd, CEO of Geometry Global in London, and Chris Macdonald, CEO of McCann in New York, have been brave enough to try out the Mote system in their substantial agencies. Sarah was a star in the early days, and I am really grateful to her for conducting the prototype Meeting System Survey, and allowing me to share the results with you - my readers. Alex Lubar and Mike Tsang of McCann New York have been enthusiastic Mote pioneers and cheerleaders.

Among other valued collaborators, I would like to mention Kirk Vallis at Google, Kate Howe and Simon Calvert at Gyro, Tom Wong, Johnny Wright and Mike Longhurst at McCann London, Mike Dodds at Proximity and Michael Islip at Digitas LBi.

I much appreciate my old friend and client Martin Riley writing a kind Foreword, and the brave souls who have endorsed the book as something of value.

The amount of experience and insights passed on to me directly and indirectly by these and other friends has been invaluable.

I have also huge learned much from a wide swathe

of academics, experts and business writers – meeting specialists, philosophers, psychologists and thought leaders across a wider canvass. The contribution of these authorities is appropriately referenced. But I would like to single out four gurus in particular: Marshall Goldsmith, Tony Crabbe, Daniel Levitin, and Roman Krznaric.

And when developing a new idea, I would like to say how much I owe to the schoolmasters at St Edward's School and the tutors at Jesus College Oxford for encouraging me to be impatient with received wisdom and default settings.

My publisher Matthew Smith has simply been outstanding again, this time at the helm of Urbane Publications, as a guide, a skilled editor, and above all as chief cheerleader for this project.

'**Mote**' has benefited greatly from being illustrated, and my thanks go to Tim Cordell (interestingly a copywriter who draws!), for his creativity, cartoons, caricatures, and extremely co-operative way of working.

I am also hugely grateful for the loyal support of my remarkable assistant Tania Zimmerman, for helping to keep the show on the road while I have been researching and writing.

Finally a big thank you to Lotta Malm Hallqvist for all her encouragement, as well as her colleagues at Cheil Worldwide for organising a launch party for the book.

FOREWORD

by Martin Riley, Former CMO of the Pernod Ricard Groupe and President of the World Federation of Advertisers 2013–2015

When David first talked to me about the subject of this book it struck an immediate chord. Like so many people in business I have attended literally thousands of meetings during my career and an incalculable amount of time has been spent in meeting mode. How often do we hear the phrase 'I spend my life in meetings'?

Indeed I recall a colleague some years ago describing to his young son a typical day at the office, 'I sit around a big table and talk to people. Sometimes they are the same people and sometimes they are different. And then I come home'.

So why and how have we evolved into this state? That is one of the questions which this book addresses. There is the frightening cost to companies and the economy of wasted meetings. And of course as someone who's always worked for international organisations, I'm well aware that it is a global phenomenon. Then there is the damage that meetings do to people.

Management of time, our most precious commodity in business and in private life, lies at the heart of this dilemma.

It may be 'un probleme des riches', as the French say, in that successful companies and well paid executives at all levels can work this way. Although they may feel frustration, it is not yet recognised as a crisis. There doesn't seem to be a burning platform, except that time is finite and we should not waste it. There is also the damage that people can do to meetings, and David and his cartoonist colleague illustrate how bad this can be – amusingly, but you will recognise some old friends.

Is there a more efficient way of getting to a decision- and then acting on it?

When we say, 'that was a good meeting', what do we actually mean? How do we evaluate the process and the outcome? David counsels strongly against having too many people in the room. He advocates starting the meeting small, only adding people sparingly when they can make a contribution, and letting them go when they have delivered it. He doesn't agree with the 'delegate' approach to a classic strategic or project meeting. He sees the people around the table as members of a team, focused on a goal, and dedicated to working collaboratively together.

How do we avoid moving seamlessly from one meeting to the other during our working day and then realising we can't remember exactly what we agreed, and have no time to act upon it anyway?

What David has identified is the lack of preparation we all suffer for the Meeting Culture that has infiltrated and come to dominate business life. We expect people to absorb this culture, like osmosis, but what if we had a more systematic approach? What if people were more conscious of what is required of them in different kinds of meetings, before they walk into the room?

There are formal and informal meetings; there are internal and external meetings; there are customer and supplier meetings. In some of these meetings we are in 'send message' mode and in others 'receive message' mode. Is our mind set and anticipation the same in all cases? What kind of preparation is required, and by whom? Who leads?

This book offers a roadmap to all meeting participants, which is virtually everybody who has a job. We are given a structure to consider, and encouraged to try putting ourselves in the shoes of others, as a way of avoiding unnecessary conflict. This is a tool and image we can keep in our mind's eye as a reference to ensure we differentiate input from output and move towards a decision and achieve a result.

Mote looks like a really significant innovation to me, and having worked with David for twelve years or so, I'm not surprised at him coming up with a radical remedy for a vexing problem. The 5 Principles of Mote provide insight, illumination and a philosophical grounding for a new meeting regime. I believe Mote can offer a solution to the challenges and dilemmas of our meeting dominated working culture. It should also offer an answer to the key question:

'What do we have to do to make this a good meeting?'

Martin Riley, April 2015

"A meeting? You bet I would!"

Chapter 1

THE JOY OF MEETING

'The pain of parting is nothing to the joy of meeting again'
Charles Dickens, *Nicholas Nickleby*

Meeting? Joy?

The two words don't sit easily together, at least in a business context. There is so much to criticise in the way meetings have taken over our lives – and not in a good way. In this book I set out to analyse the meetings phenomenon, and to spell out what I believe has gone wrong, and why. I look at the statistics on how much time and money is wasted in bad meetings, and the role of organisations in allowing up to half the working lives of their best people to be sacrificed in largely ineffective spells sitting around a conference table. I look at the collateral damage to the lives and careers of these people, aka you, me, us. I also examine the way in which meeting participants (yes that's us again, I'm afraid) have contributed to bad meetings by unhelpful behaviour and etiquette.

But, as I make clear on the front cover, this is an optimistic book, a positive book, and hopefully a practical book. The development of Mote – a better way of managing and participating in meetings – is good news for the vast majority of us who want to work collaboratively and successfully with our colleagues. This is a book for companies. It is a book for the managers in those organisations responsible for running meetings. And if you are one of the millions of us whose job requires you to be in meetings every day, it is also very much a book for you.

I think we'd all agree that meetings can be improved. But what if we could not just improve them, but replace them with better practice, more productivity and a satisfying and enjoyable experience? Perhaps joy in meetings is not such a pie in the sky idea after all! Mote is not just a better meeting, but a better way for us all to work together. Psychologists tell us that nearly everything we enjoy doing together, we do better.

Why am I committed to devising a new way to do meetings? It has quite a lot to do with the thousands of meetings I have attended!

Meetings are the way the modern business world has chosen to work together. But they are deeply flawed, and I believe that we all need to understand the extent of the problem, why things go wrong, and what we can do about the situation. It is important to help both companies and individuals become much more professional meeting organisers and participants.

This book is also a direct result of the extensive research and interview programme I conducted before writing *DECIDE: Better Ways of Making Better Decisions* (Kogan

Page, 2013). Meetings play an important role at various stages of what I term the Smart Decisions Approach. Decision makers need to interact with experts and stakeholders to assess the reward/risk implications of the various options before them. Meetings are also valuable to closely define opportunities and problems, as well as more generally to exercise a degree of democracy. In *Decide,* I highlighted the shortcomings of the classic 60 minute meeting – too many people in the room, not enough time for everyone to be heard, and participants still mulling over what happened in their last meeting, and starting to worry about the next one.

Sadly poor organisation and management are only two of the problems with meetings. There is overwhelming evidence of widespread lapses in good behaviour and etiquette, as well as incontrovertible evidence that in most organisations there are far too many meetings, and not enough time for people to recover, work effectively, and achieve a healthy work/life balance.

At the macro level, the situation is more serious still. There are authentic headline estimates valuing wasted time in meetings in the UK at a staggering £50bn a year. There is an unbelievable toll on the time of the brightest and the best – all countries, all sectors, all businesses. In trying to sort out the meetings crisis, the goal is not simply best practice or upskilling the executive classes. We are talking about helping everyone to become 'better at meetings', and to create positive collaborations. This is a chance to make a very significant contribution to business life – saving millions of people hours sacrificed to unproductive meetings. Companies need fewer, better meetings, and that can only be achieved if we all rethink our attitude to meetings.

Something must be done!

My conclusion after nearly 50 years at work (and in 40-odd countries, so this is far from a purely UK perspective), is that government, business, and organisations of all kinds are bedevilled by a hugely inefficient way of bringing people together. There are so many meetings in our lives that to be in a meeting has become the routine, keeping even more people away from useful work. They are mostly attended by too many people, and there are too many items on the agenda. Often there is disappointingly little by way of outcome – except the fixing of further meetings.

I have seen some hopeful signs in my daily working life

For more than a quarter of a century, I have facilitated what might be termed 'managed meetings' in my role as an advisor to very large brand owners. I have been a privileged observer as major brand owners invited the world's best communications agencies to pitch for launches, innovations, new looks and new business. The most talented performers – in both agencies and client companies – are outstanding in one important area: bringing about transformations and managing change. The stakes are invariably high, and the transformation has always to be planned in real time alongside the ongoing marketing of the existing brand. The process is relentlessly dynamic and it has inspired me to respect dynamism, and look for its application in all organisations.

Dynamism needs individuals with ideas and the drive to make them happen – people who are good at spotting and realising opportunities, and who are astute at recognising problems and solving them. But dynamism also needs teamwork – people with synergistic and complementary skills, experts with differentiated abilities, and teams with the joint application and determination to manage and deliver change. To make teams work, you need collaboration, and to drive collaboration you need meetings; managed meetings to deliver results. When the pressure is on innovation is the order of the day – and that's where Mote comes in.

My mission

My focus is to destabilise, marginalise, and utterly undermine **BAD** meetings! Organisations have a constant requirement for projects, change management, and important decisions. I am a reformer at heart – not just a critic – so I have been searching for a way of working together that is superior to the meeting as we know it.

I have been hugely stimulated by the outstanding psychologists, philosophers, and business academics currently shedding light on how business people tick – individually and collectively – and the factors that limit potential. I have also had access to invaluable new research into the emotional side of change management, which has heightened my determination to focus on the fragile strengths and many weaknesses of meetings in business today.

We all need an innovative style of meeting. Meetings are vital. How else can 21st century men and women work and do business together? But I am so convinced the way we do meetings now is a disaster that I set out to design a new meeting system.

I call my 'Super Meeting' a Mote. It's a new kind of dynamic meeting specifically designed to help organisations drive change, solve problems, realise opportunities, bring projects to fruition, and enable successful decisions. It has also been designed for people, for you, for me, and for any of us who need to think together and work together.

The essentials of Mote technique and values will work in all meetings. The Mote philosophy – the Spirit of Mote – will materially improve the way organisations work and how people work in and with these organisations. Mote can become a guiding principle for all workplace behaviour.

This is your chance to meet Mote, understand Mote, apply Mote – and discover the joy of being a Moter!

◆ MOTEBITE

"If you had to identify, in one word, the reason why the human race has not achieved, and never will achieve, its full potential, that word would be 'meetings'."
– Dave Barry

Mote is the change, Mote enables achievement

"Shall we call a meeting...and if so, what shall we call it?"

Chapter 2

MEETINGS ARE NOT ALL CREATED EQUAL – MEET THE SUPER SIX!

We have become very used to calling meetings, running meetings, being invited to meetings, and indeed complaining about the time we spend in meetings. It is easy to forget that meetings come in many shapes and sizes.

We spend weeks and months in meetings (years if you add up all the meetings you attend in a career), and almost no one has a good word to say about them. Unfortunately meetings do not generally work very well but our diaries are full of them – frustrating meetings, counterproductive meetings, meetings that far from moving things forward, serve to hold us back and slow us down. It's often easy to list the issues with meetings:

- Too many meetings
- Meetings that go on too long
- Meetings with too many people
- Meetings missing the right people
- Meetings with the wrong people present
- Meetings at the wrong time
- Meetings that are poorly managed

- Meetings lacking the correct facilities
- Meetings without agendas or with unrealistic agendas
- Meetings that do not progress projects or produce decisions
- Bad meeting etiquette
- Bad meeting behaviour

These problems are 'meeting traps', named after the decision traps that can bedevil decision making. In *DECIDE* I identify the 60 minute meeting as a serious stumbling block:

'It is the average time for a meeting. We can streamline business decision making by making meetings super-productive. The numerous 60 minute slots we have in our daily and weekly schedules deserve to be given more attention and planning, and to have much more useful outcomes than is often the case.'

Why are we so critical about something so fundamental to our working lives? If meetings are as bad as everyone says, why haven't we done anything about it?

Have you ever realised that there is no one word for someone who attends a meeting? 'Attendee' sounds a bit pompous. Look for a synonym, and 'participant' is really the only contender, which again is slightly pretentious. Neither French nor the other Latin-based languages can produce one single word either. The Germans have a word but it is less than accessible – *Tagungsteilnehmer*.

Is it that we love meetings so little that we haven't even

produced affectionate slang or jargon to chat about them? 'Conference room', 'agenda' (the Latin for what has to be done) and 'minutes' are all slightly cold terms. I don't know who coined the phrase 'A meeting is where you take minutes and waste hours', but it is a widely held view. There has also been remarkably little written about meetings on the academic front. There are a host of blog sites, and relatively few books, most of which start with the viewpoint that we are stuck with lots of meetings, attended by lots of people, and all you can do is make them slightly less painful.

◆ MOTEBITE

One of the most surprising things about meetings is how little we talk about them compared to how much time we spend in them. Meetings seem to be at the opposite end of this scale from say politics, football, show business, food or sex!

Introducing the Super Six

Let's distinguish between different types of meeting. There six basic types:

• *Assembly Meetings*
  Meetings that serve to supply our basic human
  need for contact and interaction. Meetings of people
  who have been elected – to everything from the UN
  General Assembly to parliaments, councils, boards
  and committees. English writer and philosopher GK
  Chesterton (1874-1936) wrote, 'I've searched all the parks

in all the cities and found no statues of committees'. Like meetings, committees get a bad press, but as we shall see later, there are ways of helping them function better.

- *Briefing Meetings*
  Meetings to tell people things, and provide information. Usually, but not always, top down. Something has happened or been decided, and this is what we are going to do about it. Understood? Any questions? It is obviously better, if possible, to **tell** people something important. Even a quick meeting is preferable to a few words in an email or on a notice board. In my AAI world, briefing meetings (provided by clients for agencies) kick-start the creative process, and are crucial

- *Team Meetings*
  Meetings of project teams. Meetings as a management device and also as an exercise in democracy

- *Learning Meetings*
  Meetings to learn – in schools, universities and colleges, arguably also services in church/temple/mosque etc

- *Selling Meetings*
  Where one organisation or individual is selling to another. Also 'selling up' meetings within companies

- *Dynamic Meetings*
  Meetings with a purpose: eg creating and managing change, driving projects. They are meetings designed to achieve a decision. Also frequently known as Strategic Meetings

My principal preoccupation is with this last set of dynamic meetings that are designed to produce or lead to a decision. All organisations rely on meetings to develop, process and ratify decisions. We meet so that we can work together and make decisions. Decision making is the cornerstone of high performance companies, a vital skill for successful people and meetings are the essential vehicle for managing decision making in organisations. Unfortunately these meetings in particular are often dysfunctional and have become the bane of corporate existence.

Why meetings are important

They are important above all to help decision making. Each meeting should be designed to take us one or more steps along the road to a significant decision. Meetings are important to enable information, data, news, and developments (whether positive or not) to be shared and disseminated. Meetings are also often used to bring in expert advisers. We use meetings to ask (find out information and views), especially among stakeholders, and to persuade, motivate, negotiate, and to tell (instruct, communicate policy, decisions etc).

Meetings also serve to supply our basic human need for contact and interaction – which is important if we are anchored for hours at a work station. And even when it's not possible to meet in person, email, phones and video and audio conferencing allow us to meet remotely.

Having clever people in a meeting room does not necessarily produce great results or good decisions

Shouldn't decision taking be about using meetings to engage colleagues and refine the final decision so it is as good as possible? If only!

There are three main problems here.

Firstly, clever people don't always behave in a clever way, or contribute constructively to a meeting. Too many 'smart ideas' can cancel each other out if the group is not well-balanced. Putting a group of talented people together doesn't guarantee the success of a meeting; any more than having the ability to make good decisions means you are a consistently good decision-maker. When clever people perform in an un-clever way that definitely qualifies as a meeting trap. We might call it the **Cleverness Illusion**.

Secondly, the meeting can evolve into a social occasion, a chance to escape the desk. I read recently someone describing the meeting as 'a practical alternative to work: you get to meet other people, feel important, and impress your colleagues – all in work time'. Simply putting people together is no guarantee of success. The meeting needs to be organised and led.

Thirdly, the average meeting is ineffective because it doesn't necessarily allow the people around the table to work effectively. For example, if there are too many people in the room it is difficult for all individuals to make much of a contribution, which leads to limited airtime and general frustration. Or there could be too many items on the agenda, not giving the key issues enough coverage.

All meetings – no exceptions – are called because one person has an idea, a plan, a possible way forward, and needs to engage with people who can either help move it forward or approve it. Bear this in mind – ideas and plans come before meetings, not out of them.

◆ MOTEBITE

Clever people don't always behave in a clever way, or contribute constructively to a meeting.

What are meeting outputs and outcomes?

Let's revisit the 'super six'.

- *Assembly (representation by election, parliaments, councils, committees, management boards)*
  - Output: proposing, opposing, debating and passing motions
  - Outcome: legislation, board resolutions etc
- *Briefing (telling people things and providing information)*
  - Output: authority informs people
  - Outcome: people are informed and have the chance to ask questions
- *Team (as a management device and also as an exercise in democracy)*
  - Output: Team members update each other, usually under supervision of authority

- Outcome: Team members get on with their work, armed with latest data and possibly revised goals
- *Learning (schools, universities and colleges, training, and arguably religious meetings: church/temple/mosque etc)*
  - Output: authority instructs people
  - Outcome: people learn, worship etc
- *Selling (one organisation selling to another, and 'selling up' meetings within companies)*
  - Output: seller attempts to sell to buyer
  - Outcome: buyer decides to buy – or not
- *Dynamic (meetings with a purpose, creating and managing change, driving projects -meetings designed to make progress, realise opportunities, solve problems, make decisions)*
  - Output: team / group members work together to achieve nominated goal – eg solve problem, define opportunity, reach decision, progress project
  - Outcome: problem solved, opportunity realised, decision reached, project finalised

Meetings are different – but are the problems essentially the same?

Assembly Meetings

The fundamental weakness of the Assembly Meeting is also its strength. A parliament, council or committee has to be a certain size to fulfil its basic function – being representative. 650 MPs is a big meeting by any standard; too big in fact for the Chamber of the House of Commons to accommodate them all at the same time. Indeed 650 seems a lot of delegates to represent 60m people (at 92k per member), particularly when compared, for instance, to the 435 members of the House of Representatives who look after the interests of the 320m population of the USA (736k people per member). But try the States of Guernsey; that has 45 deputies for 65k people (1444 people per member)!

The positive driver of such traditions is democracy. Voters entrust their tribunes with governance, law making, redressing wrongs, and planning for the future by delegating authority to them. Big meetings are an inevitable consequence, and it is hard to criticise MPs for turning up, even if proceedings in the Commons can come across as turgid, boring and chaotic by turns. As we shall see later, there are some improvements to be made to assembly meetings, but more in terms of behaviour and etiquette. Managing expectations is important in assembly meetings. Delegates are often elected as party members or at least supporters of one point of view rather than another. There are many possible outcomes in these sessions, but instances of opponents persuading each other of their point of view are rarer than hen's teeth. In contrast to a dynamic meeting, persuasion, advocacy and efforts to achieve consensus are frequently frustrated. It is not so much a weakness of assemblies as a confirmation of human nature!

Briefing Meetings

There is a big plus to these meetings. It is far preferable for management to communicate live with staff, as compared to sending emails or posting notices. It is more democratic, more personal and more interactive.

Conventionally briefing meetings are usually of short duration. It is hard to argue with the basic principle that it is the ideal format for communicating one piece of information to everyone simultaneously.

In my world of advertising agencies and their clients, I have a strong preference for arranging individual briefings for each agency in a new business process. It obviously takes longer for a client to provide five briefings as opposed to one mass briefing, but the mass briefing makes it difficult for each agency team to ask the specific questions they want to in front of their rivals. Individual briefings are far more motivating and effective.

Essentially there is no effectiveness problem with classic announcement meetings, provided 'management' is frank in its dissemination of information, and 'staff' are co-operative and engaged.

Team Meetings

Team meetings as we know them today have been heavily influenced by the software development industry. In 2001, seventeen influential software developers from different organisations published their *'Manifesto for Agile Software Development'*, saying, 'We are uncovering better ways of developing software by doing it and helping others do it. Through this work we have come to value':

- **Individuals and interactions** over Processes and tools
- **Working software** over Comprehensive documentation
- **Customer collaboration** over Contract negotiation
- **Responding to change** over Following a plan

Their vision was to replace the traditional 'Waterfall' process (which worked on the basis of the descriptions above) with a more iterative, flexible and swift way of working (hence 'Agile').

Later came the 'Scrum' movement, which itself generated 'Sprints'. Scrums have come to mean daily, fifteen minute stand-up team meetings, to measure progress in Sprints, which are units of time signifying development stages of somewhere between a week and a month in duration.

Again, numbers are a given. If it is a team meeting, as many as possible of the team need to be there. The overriding purpose of a team meeting is for a leader to make sure all projects are proceeding to plan, and for the team members to check they are personally on track and share problems or queries. To work well, team meetings need to be regular, brief, efficient and lively. Expert assessments of the average attention span vary from just under half an hour to rather less than a full hour. Aiming at thirty minutes for a team meeting makes sense for both leader and team.

Critics of repetitive team meetings suggest updating by email if activity is less than usual or regular attendees have to be elsewhere. There are also concerns around using team sessions for praising or criticising individuals or small teams. It can be a good idea to praise in public, but there is an obvious downside in terms of demotivating others. Similarly there is almost always a better management choice than issuing a public criticism or dressing down.

Learning Meetings

It is interesting that there is little general criticism of learning meetings in contrast to other types of meeting. Learning meetings usually have an appropriate venue, a start and end time, a leader, a defined list of participants, and most importantly a set of conventions and rules that determine how the session should run. Also expectations are managed as learning meetings are almost always one of a series, so there should not be over-ambitious goals. Equally the attendees are there to learn or participate, which provides greater benefits than for those attending a conventional meeting.

There is much to learn from learning meetings. They have certain characteristics which would be beneficial in other kinds of meeting, specifically:

- Series of learning meetings (to deliver a course or syllabus), broken down into individual sessions. Easy to understand goals of both series and sessions
- Start and end times – and therefore duration of meeting – set in stone
- Meeting duration usually standard (at forty-five or

sixty minutes), with provision for double periods as a convenient alternative to two separate sessions. From the point of view of both 'teacher' and 'pupil' there are obvious advantages of regular time frames, which are predictable and not too long. Everyone soon becomes accustomed to cadence and rhythm

- Breaks built between sessions, periods, lectures, and services, to provide both teacher and pupil with recovery time

Selling Meetings

There is a difference with other meetings in that the participants divide into buyers and sellers. The meeting might be brief if the projected sale is largely transactional and a one-off. Alternatively if the meeting is just one stage in a significant mutual decision process, both the meeting and the series of meetings may well be protracted. There is a real difference between a seller persuading someone to buy (where the alternative outcome is essentially no sale) and an agreed negotiation or formal selection, where one seller is going to win and the others lose. This difference informs how the meetings are likely to go. Transactional sales meetings can be short and adversarial whereas pitch meetings can be well-planned, engaging and consensual.

Dynamic Meetings

These are the strategic meetings which need the best possible conditions, optimum performance, and an absence of meeting traps. A significant offender is 'Stakeholder

Saturation'. This is one of the most disappointing threats to the dynamic meeting. It seems so logical in a change management environment to recruit as many stakeholders as possible and gather them in a conference room. Won't that guarantee maximum momentum for change? Sadly not. Show me a room full of stakeholders, and I will quickly be able to identify the ones determined to resist the change proposed. It is as serious a problem as the Cleverness Illusion.

And the meeting traps don't end there. The dynamic meeting, which is in many ways the most important and potent meeting of all, is particularly susceptible to things going wrong. I have concentrated on dynamic meetings because of their extraordinary potential. Meetings are how we work together. When the task is to drive a vital project, to facilitate decision making, and to bring about change, simply having the best people is not enough. It is vital to find the best way to harness their talent and flair, use their experience, and work as a team.

◆ MOTEBITE

Dynamic Meetings are key to transformations and change management, but each of the other 'Super Six' meetings needs to be used and managed better

"We can't go on meeting like this."

Chapter 3

WE CAN'T GO ON MEETING LIKE THIS

John Kenneth Galbraith once said, 'meetings are indispensable when you don't want to do anything.'

Everyone knows that meetings can be deeply frustrating. Many of us seem to spend half our life in meetings. Some of us actually do. But no one seems to have any idea how to make meetings more productive and effective. Until Mote.

'Meetings Bloody Meetings' – now the biggest obstacle to progress faced by businesses all over the world

What's the greatest challenge for business leaders? Profitability? No. Productivity? No. Sustainability? No. Communications? No. Diversity? No. Red tape? No.

I'm talking about The Meeting, the dysfunctional and villainous consumer of people and time. It should be the pathway to decision making, the engine of progress, and the translator of individual talent into collective excellence. Instead meetings in most organisations achieve little, demotivate participants, and waste both time and money.

Wasteful, inefficient meetings pose an enormous cost to both companies and the executives condemned to suffer in them. In the UK in a single year the cost of wasted meeting time is estimated at an astonishing £50bn; that's over 3% of GDP! And it is not just a time and money problem because bad meetings contribute to stress and poor health. They have a significant effect on life/work balance, by eating into work time and obliging executives to work longer hours, travel more, and see less of their families.

It is clear that this 'waste' is caused by far too many meetings that last too long, have too many people in the room, and boast a widespread lack of professional meeting managers. Organisations are literally throwing away huge amounts of time and money.

Yet you cannot make business decisions or implement them without meetings. This frustration seems to have made meetings the bane of most people's working lives. Here are the Top Ten most obvious meeting mistakes:

1. Poor leadership
2. Ineffective follow up and implementation
3. Failure to set a goal for the meeting
4. Too many items on the agenda
5. Too many attendees.
6. Not enough time spent on preparation
7. No effort to profile participants, so as to get a balanced team.
8. Loud voices allowed to dominate
9. People overtalking and interrupting
10. Too much confrontational behaviour and tone

And those are just features of the old fashioned face-to-face meeting, with everyone in one room. If they seem to work increasingly less efficiently, what price the ubiquitous conference call? Dominant and persistent voices rule. Conference calls for the most part are all output, with everyone queuing up to speak. Any listening is passive and grudging. I feel that conference calls don't work well even as status updates. As a forum for decision making they are quite simply hopeless. Video conferencing and Skype work better, but often suffer from many of the defects of 'live' meetings. Peoples' preference for social media and one-to-one communications has also made traditional meetings unpopular.

Is there anything that can be done? This isn't a quick fix. The answer, like the meeting, needs to be more dynamic.

Let's start with the punch line

We are all pushed for time, and trying to pack so much into one mega-busy day after another. Maybe it would be sensible to start with the punch line. Have we got the time and patience to wade through all the intermediate stages? We watch Match of the Day or record the game, and fast forward through to the last ten minutes. We record soaps, skip the early stages and the ads, and zip through to the denouement. When you think about it, we are brought up very iteratively. Every lesson and course at school, every book, every TV programme, every movie, every play, every set of instructions, every recipe, every game of football, starts at the beginning and proceeds steadily through to the final act, the last page and 'The End'.

Why invite 15 people to a 90 minute meeting when none of them know what the outcome is going to be? Why not plan the session and at least give them a hint of what you want to happen? Time is money, and unexpected outcomes are not the ideal in the impatient business world. When it comes to meetings, doesn't it make sense for the organiser(s) to plan the desired outcome, share that with the participants, and collaboratively work through the 'whys', 'hows' and 'what do we do next'?

There IS an answer to the meetings nightmare, and it's called Mote. I have been working on the Mote meeting system for nearly two years, but it was very recently that I realised Mote is more, far more, than a simple process, or just a 'right way' or running meetings. But to begin let's substantiate the claim that we can't go on meeting like this.

How bad is the problem?

In 2012 Epson published a survey showing that staff in Small and Medium Sized Enterprises (SMEs) in the UK were wasting an average of 2 hours 39 minutes every week in meetings. This represented a loss of 13m productive hours a week. Epson estimated the annual loss to the economy of this at £26bn, or 1.7% of GDP.

To reiterate, this was just in SMEs, where there tend to be fewer meetings than in big companies. SMEs represent just under 50% of total private sector employment in the UK, so the Epson figures would suggest that the cost of wasted time in meetings could be well over £50bn in a single year.

Management Today reported that the average office worker spends 16 hours in meetings every week (37% of all working hours). And that is the *average*. For senior managers that percentage rises to approximately 50% of their time in meetings. I discovered a tidal flow of US statistics from a sea of websites too numerous to be able to mention them all individually. If you are still in any doubt as to the seriousness of the deep-seated malaise undermining the meetings industry, just Google 'Time wasted in meetings'.

For example, there was an Industry Week survey of 2000 managers (also in 2012) which focused on wasted meetings rather than wasted time in all meetings. This came up with a cost figure for the US of $37bn. One Fortune 50 company estimated their losses in wasted meetings at $75m a year. Another corporation costed their aggregated wasted meeting time globally at $3.7bn! Most of this is based on average salary totals, but there must be an additional factor in the cost of travelling to meetings, accommodation, subsistence and so on.

Here are some other frightening stats from the US:

- Somewhere between 11m and 17m formal business meetings every day
- 25-30% of time spent in meetings wasted
- Average staff member spending 37% of working time in meetings (interestingly exactly the same as in the UK)

- Average worker only effectively working three days a week in aggregate
- 47% quoted meetings as the biggest waste of their time
- 62 meetings attended every month...
- ...and 96% of people miss at least one meeting in a month
- 31 unproductive meeting hours every month
- Status update meetings – 70% say they don't help them get work done, and 67% say they spend up to 4 hours a week preparing for the next status meeting
- 63% of the meetings have no formal agendas
- Over 70% of people bring other work to meetings
- 39% admit to dozing off from time to time
- 91% daydream
- 60% take notes to appear as if that they are listening
- It takes less than 8 seconds for ideas, proposals and suggestions to be criticised
- Average employee checks their email 36 times in an hour (sometimes during meetings), and takes 16 minutes to refocus after a lengthy email session

The Center for Work Life Policy says that the average professional work week has expanded steadily with many people working 60-70 hours every week. Al Pittampalli, author of *Read This Before Our Next Meeting* says, 'We're now addicted to meetings that insulate us from the work we should be doing'. Influential blogger Ray Williams wrote in *Wired for Success*, 'Meeting activities expand to fill the time available'. He advised, 'Cancel 50 percent of your meetings and you'll get more work done'!

Industry Week called the $37bn cost of wasted time 'the great white collar crime', and expert opinion suggests that this figure was substantially understated.

Let's look at some of the background to this

Self-evidently there are more meetings than there used to be, apparently to generate lesser results. A recent MCI (US small businesses association) survey reported that 46% of respondents said they attend more meetings than a year ago. It is probable that the overwhelming switch from private offices to open plan workplaces, with everyone seated at work stations, has stimulated this sharp growth in meetings. A lot of informal conversations took place in private offices. Now these sessions have translated into meetings.

Meetings last longer. They cause frustration. They eat into work time. They force particularly senior managers to work longer, to stay later in the office, and to take work home.

A good question is why so few organisations, knowing all or most of the above, have not taking any serious action. Maybe this is another – ironic – opportunity cost of the fatigue and frustration caused by so many unproductive meetings. Could it be the case that the very people who could improve the situation are too tired and too busy to make the effort?

Of course it would be a mistake to assume that none of us want meetings. We often say and hear 'Let's fix a meeting' when there's a new piece of work or a project to be discussed. Inevitably the discussion will be on hold till the meeting takes place, and that meeting date may well be postponed if a key player cannot make it. More delay. Less resolution of the problem. Less identification and realisation of the opportunity.

There are also some constructive statistics:

- It is estimated that a skilled facilitator can increase the productivity of a meeting by 25%
- Having a proper agenda and starting on time can reduce time spent in meetings by as much as 80%
- An hour of planning will save 10 hours of doing

The problem with meetings is particularly serious if we believe that organisations should foster a strong decision-making culture

I came to meetings fresh from tackling decision making in *DECIDE*, and challenging the conventional wisdom that successful deciders are all left brain thinkers who rely on logic and reason. They aren't. Gut feel is vital, and as many decisions are made by groups in meeting rooms as by individuals outside them, often after overnight reflection.

Decision making is the cornerstone of high performance companies, and a vital skill for successful people. Meetings are essential to manage decision making in organisations, but they are often dysfunctional and have become the bane of corporate existence. We need to improve decision making by re-engineering the meeting. Meetings play a critical part in confirming and ratifying decisions. Meetings are after all the way we have come to work together, and are therefore indispensable to our decision making process.

It is impossible to deliver decision making in companies without meetings – but it is not as easy as that

The familiar ritual of 'the meeting' happens in every organisation, worldwide, all the time. While I am writing this piece and while you are reading it, and indeed when we are both asleep, millions of meetings will be in progress somewhere on the planet.

Every company is packed with highly qualified people. Isn't decision making basically a question of harnessing these skills and using meetings to engage colleagues and refine the final decision so it is as good as possible? Unfortunately having the ability to make good decisions doesn't mean that you are a consistently good decision-maker.

The fundamental problem however lies in the meeting itself, and the gap between what it is meant to achieve, and what tends to happen in reality. Meetings are a chore; it is hard to get people to raise their game for a meeting where a decision is essential. Very few achieve what they are supposed to. And decisions are therefore thin on the ground. The meeting has retained its roles as a forum for discussion, and a way of keeping people informed. But as a general rule today we don't expect meetings to produce decisions and positive outcomes.

Why have meetings become so ineffective? Sadly we find everywhere that there is a lack of process and discipline in the way meetings are run. Sometimes that is down to a lack of pre-planning. Or it can be a basic lack of leadership. There may be a too hierarchical an approach which doesn't help democracy within the team. It is not uncommon to come across bad manners and behaviour. And how often have we watched meetings go off-track because of highly selective provision of data and information? It is so easy for dominant personalities to bias proceedings in favour of their own ideas and suggestions.

◆ MOTEBITE

There are so many meetings about inconsequential issues, that it is hard to get people to raise their game for a meeting where a decision is essential

There may also be challenges which stem from modern cultural influences. People seem to be happier contacting their friends and associates remotely rather than actually meeting. Look how much time we spend emailing, phoning, texting, and using social media. When we do meet, we prefer one-to-one encounters. And thanks to the volume of words and thoughts and ideas that we now routinely get down on paper in reports, emails, blogs, tweets and so on, there's a highly developed sense of personal brand. That doesn't help democracy and teamwork.

To make real progress we need to help people become outstanding decision makers, and that isn't going to happen unless we also work out a better way of doing meetings.

To sum up, most businesses are reliant on high-quality decision making, and there is clear evidence that determined individuals with clear goals make better decision makers. But badly run meetings don't help. We need to find better ways of running meetings to bring about a major improvement in decision making.

How do we go about making business decisions, and how do we use meetings during that process?

Great decisions usually come from a good decision making process. Setting up in a rigorous way shortens the odds on making a good decision. So much in decision making is connected with change management, where the key question tends to be: what is the ultimate goal? Until everyone has agreed on the goal, it is unsafe to move on to the decision process. So one or more meetings at the outset – to discuss and codify the goal – are essential.

The Smart Decisions Approach

Here are the ten steps leading to confirming, but not implementing, a decision. The process is described in the first person singular, but obviously collaboration, discussion and development require other people and, yes, meetings.

1. Am I sure what the opportunity is? Or am I sure what the problem is?

2. If it's an opportunity, have I identified it correctly, and do I know how I am going to take advantage of it?

3. If it's a problem, do I know precisely what it is, and how I am going to solve it?

4. So what is my goal? This must be exactly what I am looking to my decision to achieve. Unless everyone concerned with a decision knows what the desired outcome is, you cannot assess the wisdom of a decision or particular course of action. A politician can choose between different goals: winning the election, reducing taxes, becoming Prime Minister. The decision might be what to put in the election manifesto. A general might have decided in his own mind to try and recapture a town lost last week. But what's the goal?

5. Is pursuing this goal one for me to tackle on my own, or is it a team task – in which case have we got the right team on the case?

6. Having agreed on the opportunity or problem, and set a goal, it is then time to look at options: how many possible answers are there? What are these options? Are we sure we have explored all the meaningful ones?

7. Is there enough data and information to analyse each of the options, and can we get more if needs be? We need to leave reasonable time here (if available) for gathering and analysing information and intelligence. Control what we can, and we must do our best to predict what we can't

8. Have we looked at the upsides and downsides of each

option? For each option we need to write down the best upside (highest reward) and the worst potential downside (biggest risk)

9. If it isn't immediately obvious what is the most compelling route, first look at the worst downside, and eliminate that route, unless the upside is particularly alluring. Then look at the upsides in order of attractiveness. We are looking for the best balance

10. What looks to be the best decision?

Steps 1-3: Should have been taken care of in our advanced planning, which will inevitably have involved one or more meetings.

Step 4: Having been rigorous in interrogating the opportunity or problem, we should be in shape to define the goal, in pursuit of which we have to make a decision. Committing to a goal is absolutely essential. Neither capitalising on an opportunity nor solving a problem is of itself going to be the goal. We have to know what we're aiming at. We have to meet to debate, interrogate, and agree.

Steps 5-10: The essence of the rational side of the Smart Decision process. Every step is important for all decisions except the ones that have to be made instantly, or very quickly. A meeting will be needed at each of the stages.

We still need to think about how best to communicate the decision, because a decision only becomes real when it goes public. We also need to think about how to implement it, initially and ongoing, which will inevitably involve feedback, more intelligence, and more decisions.

Vitally we must also provide for gut feel before making the decision. How do we do this? Well, one of the options will almost certainly have been more attractive, as opposed to more logical. Even when we are at our most rigorous, it is difficult to be completely cold and analytical. Just as steps 1-10 will have given us a winner *in the mind*, we will almost certainly also have a winner *in the heart*. Hopefully – but by no means always – the same one.

An additional part to the Smart Decisions Approach allows for gut feel, and requires its own meeting sequence.

Steps 11-15 work like this:

11. If there is one route that is obviously the best, sleep on it. How do you feel about it the next morning? Don't be too rational. Now's the time to trust gut feel, having set up the process in a logical way. Meet to confirm

12. Or if there are two possible decisions, spend a day thinking about the first, and sleep on it. Then the next day, think about the second option, and sleep on that. How do you feel about the one against the other? Again, trust gut feel

13. Meet to decide. Then the decision must be communicated to everyone involved (unless it's a confrontational situation, where you don't want your enemy to know what you have in mind)

14. Put as much energy into implementing the decision as you did into coming up with it

15. Keep tabs on how the decision works out. Try and at least make notes, so you can learn for next time

Decisions need to be based on a balance of upside reward and downside risk, not just on a ranking of attractive upsides. My aim is to help each and every one who reads my books to become better at decision making. But within companies and organisations, being good at making decisions is a team responsibility as well. Meetings – good meetings – are essential. I shudder to think how deeply decision making could be compromised or negated by some of the 'meeting traps' featured earlier in this chapter.

Simon Calver, former CEO of Mothercare, underlined the importance of meetings in decision making when he gave his definition of competence:

- Can you make the right decision?
- Can you implement it?
- Can you bring others with you?

The Kahnemann checklist, 'before you make that big decision'

Kahnemann was looking at how we can use meetings to make sure we are on the right lines, and avoiding meeting traps and the mistakes into which they can lead us. He has a series of qualifying questions:

- Have the recommending team made errors in their own interest?

- Have they fallen in love with their own idea?
- Were there dissenting opinions that we never heard about?
- Have they used too many analogies?
- Have credible alternatives been considered?
- If they had to make this decision again in a year, what information would they want, and can they get more of it now?
- Where did the data come from?
- Is there any halo effect?
- Are they attached to past decisions?
- Is the base case too optimistic?
- Is the worst case bad enough?
- Is the team overly cautious?

Meetings designed to produce decisions require a team approach

It is quite clear that to implement decisions, we need to meet AND work in teams. Meetings are seen as an essential of business life in nearly every organisation. Why?
Because of two governing principles:

1. Hierarchy / Organisation chart: meetings are the process by which managers manage their people. They also are the 'democratic' methodology for involving peers and direct reports in decision making
2. The team ethic: meetings are the default setting for team members to work together

So it is perfectly natural and understandable that managers and executives calling dynamic meetings in an organisation should seek to fill a conference room with everyone potentially involved in shaping the output and/or managing the outcome.

The only problem is (and it is a massive problem) that filling the conference room makes it dysfunctional before the meeting has even started. It is because of the inevitable inefficiency of a room full of clever, influential people, who are also stakeholders in the status quo ante.

Quick tips from the experts

(my summary of each point in italics below)

1. "Many businesses follow an instinctive but misguided principle: the more critical the project, the more people must be thrown at it.' Ken Segall
   More brains DON'T mean better ideas. Great meetings won't happen with a room full of people

2. 'Start with small groups of smart people – and keep them small.' Ken Segall quoting Steve Jobs
   Jobs liked small hand-picked meetings with no formal agenda. He believed that a smaller group would be more focused, and that smarter people would do higher quality work

3. 'No more than ten people at a meeting.' Kristen Gil, Google
   Attending a meeting isn't a badge of honour

4. 'Conduct a pre-mortem so that you never have to

conduct a post-mortem.' Guy Kawasaki

If you have a big decision to make, start by assuming a big downside. If we were to fail, let's look at why that might happen

5. 'Consider holding a stand-up.....or walking meeting.' Rachel Emma Silverman

    Either will cut meeting time, and the walking meeting will clear heads – but there's a limit to what you can achieve in such a brief session

6. 'Every meeting starts long before you walk through the meeting room door.' Duncan Peberdy and Jane Hammersley – *BRILLIANT MEETINGS*

    Planning is everything, and will save time and money

7. 'Make everybody responsible for the meeting's success.' Alan Barker – *HOW TO MANAGE MEETINGS*

    Idle people at a meeting are a pure cost to the organisation and a source of frustration to them. A smaller number if fully engaged individuals will take responsibility

8. 'Two short better than one long.' David Pearl – *WILL THERE BE DONUTS?*

    No one benefits from a marathon meeting. Break it down into two chunks if possible

◆ MOTEBITE

Big meetings are at the heart of the problem. They are largely ineffective in decision making, and they add greatly to the catastrophic waste of time and money

"You need to cut back on the fine wines, red meats and dull meetings."

Chapter 4

THE DAMAGE MEETINGS CAN DO TO EVERYONE – AND PARTICULARLY TO OUR LIFE/WORK BALANCE

'Business' books tend to be about companies and how they can become even more efficient and dynamic. 'Life' books are all about us as individuals, and how we can become happy, fulfilled and successful. This book is for both organisations and people, and assumes it is in the interests of business as well as the individual for everyone to have a healthy balance in their lives

The Busyness of Business is a big problem

Are you busy?

After 'how are you?' it's probably the most common greeting these days. I guess we all want to be busy, and we want to be seen to be busy. So we encourage our business friends to tell us how busy they are too.

Being busy is obviously desirable economically (busy means money coming in), socially (no-one wants to be caught out watching daytime TV), and career-wise (difficult to move to a really busy job without a track record of being busy). But let's stop to think whether it is a really good idea to be busy. Or if being slightly busy or quite busy might not be better than very busy. Let's look at what being very busy means:

- Responsible job – ideally with a salary to match
- Doing well – promotion, or another company will want to hire you
- Respect all round

So far so good. But are there downsides?

- Work/life balance getting out of kilter
- Difficult to prioritise at both work and home
- Missing out on important aspects of life with family and friends – pressure on evenings, weekends, holiday times, relaxation, sleep
- Possible threat to health
- Not having time to think
- Making mistakes through being rushed
- Sitting in meeting after meeting

Let's take a look at meetings:

- What percentage of your working week is spent in meetings?
- Is that more than last year or three years ago?
- How useful are the meetings you attend?
- What would happen if you ruthlessly pruned your meeting schedule? How much time could you liberate –

every day, week, and month? What would you be able to do with the time?

- Work more?
- Work better?
- Think better and more?
- Put more time into personal life and family/friends?

Not sounding good, is it? Maybe being very busy – for hundreds of thousands if not millions of people – is a reflection of the extent to which all our working lives are dominated by meetings. And that aspect of busyness is not rewarding financially, socially or in terms of career. Nor is it likely to help the very organisation that drives the meeting regime in which you are engaged. Busy is the easy option. We are busy because other people are busy. When did someone admit they were 'unbusy'? We seem to be on a mindless search for more, and unfortunately small increments in busyness eventually have a significant effect.

I have just come out of a fantastic meeting

Really? You're right, I made it up. People simply don't talk that way, largely because fantastic meetings are rarer than hen's teeth. But people do frequently say, 'that was a really good meeting'. Why? Is it ever an objective view? Does it normally relate to outputs or likely outcomes? Often a 'good' meeting gets the title because the worst didn't happen. So much in our work lives is about expectations, and if the worst downside of a meeting was losing the business or getting fired, literally anything is better.

Meetings get a really bad press, especially when you consider how much of our lives we spend in them. It is hard to spend decades in the world of work and not get very frustrated at the sheer futility and ineffectiveness of so many meetings. The one hour meetings that fill our diaries are supposed to move projects forward and aid decision making, not diminish productivity.

There are simply too many meetings. Too many people around the table. Too many egos on display. Too little meeting technique, both from those leading meetings, and those asked to attend them. There's also confusion about what is supposed to be going on. Are meetings to inform? To update? To lobby? To persuade? To discuss? To debate? Or are meetings a process, part of the work involved in achieving a goal? In which case the end may be more important than the means. And what about meeting protocols, style and manners? How important is it to encourage civilised behaviour as well as efficiency and effectiveness?

The economist Thomas Sowell said, 'People who enjoy meetings should not be in charge of anything'. You can understand the sentiment. But if we can bring about a profound change to elevate both the performance of meetings and the degree of professional satisfaction for the participants, maybe we can make this comment irrelevant.

Minutes of the Meeting

'Before we start today, let's go through the minutes of the last meeting.'

I just wish it was minutes. Our global obsession with meetings is not costing us minutes. It's taking hours out of our day, days out of our week and weeks out of our year. I blame a meeting culture that gives us all the illusion of 'moving things on', when so often meetings serve no useful purpose, and absorb billions of people hours that otherwise might have been productive.

We probably have an effective working year of 220 days. Let's suppose that on average we are involved in two meetings a day (I wish!) – one lasting an hour, the other an hour and a half. That is 550 hours in the year spent in meetings – nearly four complete working months!

Here is a checklist to use if you feel a meeting coming on:

1. Is this meeting absolutely necessary?
2. Does it have to take place tomorrow / this week / on the 31st, or whenever?
3. Who HAS to be there?
4. What advantage is there in inviting the 'nice to haves'?
5. How long have you allocated? Is that long enough? (Or indeed too long?)
6. What's on the agenda? Can we get through all those items in the time given? Really? If we can't, which items shall we leave out?
7. Who's kicking off and managing the meeting?
8. Who's responsible for winding it up, summarising what's been achieved, writing up the conclusions / decisions?

9. Who is in charge of deciding what to do next, eg:
   - Endorsing the decision?
   - Communicating the decision?
   - Implementing the decision?
   - Or – give me strength – setting the next meeting?

10. Who is responsible for working out the optimum balance between thinking, doing and meeting?

So why have meetings become such an intrinsic business 'problem'? Here are three possible theories:

Theory One

The open plan revolution has removed the 'chat in the office' option. Quite straightforward discussions – 'how shall we handle that?', 'who does what?', 'dare we put off that briefing meeting?' – have had to be elevated to meeting status, so multiplying the volume of meetings.

Theory Two

Behaviour and manners have deteriorated to the point where many in the work place have personal styles that are so acerbic and uncooperative that they are unsuited to any recognised form of constructive debate.

Confrontational broadcast journalism has made direct attacks and interruption the default setting. Abrasiveness on reality programmes give licence to business people to behave rudely and egotistically – in fact, it is often positively encouraged.

Theory Three

Many people seem to be happier talking on the phone, texting, e-mailing or social networking than actually meeting anyone in a live encounter.

The nearly universal ability to keyboard and publish one's own material has given the class of 2015 more confidence in their opinions and indeed their personal 'brands'. Remote one-to-one interface has become the preferred way of interacting with other people. Plenty of opportunity to chat and listen and you can choose compatible chat partners in terms of personality and interests. By comparison a meeting of ten people in a conference room is a much less attractive prospect.

We have agreed that getting your life in balance requires you to attend fewer meetings – but how do you go about it?

First, look at the benefits for both the company and you of going on a meetings diet, and take the challenge seriously. You, your boss, your team all need to agree that there are benefits. What would be the gains? Are there any downsides, and what can be done to alleviate them?

What would you have to do to attend fewer meetings every week? Let's look at the Super Six:

- Assembly meetings
- Briefing meetings
- Team meetings
- Learning meetings

- Selling meetings
- Dynamic meetings

In business the Board Meeting and Board Committees account for the majority of assembly meetings, and it is difficult to cut down the frequency, although length is a valid target.

Briefing meetings tend to fall into two categories: management addressing staff 'live', as a preferable alternative to memo or email, and briefing meetings on new projects. There is no obvious time saving here.

But team meetings – unless they are of the 15/30 minutes 'Scrum' varieties – are a big time consumer.

Learning meetings (training, language classes, health and safety sessions) tend to be few and far between. They are also intrinsically useful for the most part.

In a growing organisation there is not going to be any enthusiasm for reducing the number of selling meetings – at least those where the company is selling rather being on the end of a sale!

But it is different with dynamic meetings. Important as it is to drive projects and manage change, we are all familiar with how these meetings can proliferate, take a long time to organise because of the need to line up all the stakeholders, and are often overlong, again because there are so many people in the room. And are they usually productive? No. Particularly disappointing is their contribution to decision making.

In summary, we know that meetings waste amazing amounts of time and money. We know they are very little use for making decisions. We know that they go wrong partly because often they don't fit culturally with what we want to do. We have seen what causes meeting problems – big meetings, too many meetings, meetings that last too long, and meetings that are badly organised and not managed. We have seen the hazards of poor organisation, and of bad behaviour and etiquette. We have identified both the Cleverness Illusion and Stakeholder Saturation.

These are macro problems for businesses and organisations. What about problems for individuals? How much do we think about 'busyness' and life/work balance?

We know the aggregate cost of lots of bad meetings. Do we ever calculate the opportunity cost of our being in meetings all the time? Do we push back on meeting invitations? Do we even hit 'tentative' to give us time to think? Does our organisation identify candidates to become professional meeting managers? If so, are they offered training in meeting performance?

Doesn't everyone worry about what meetings do to us?

Apparently not, particularly when you consider academic study of the subject – or rather lack of. Let's start with one of the famous of all current gurus, Nobel Prize winner Daniel Kahneman. There is only one reference to meetings in his 2011 bestseller *Thinking, Fast and Slow*. He writes in Chapter 7 about Jumping to Conclusions, and specifically about the tendency of independent judgments to be random, whereas groups will put their heads together and come up with a reasonable estimate. He writes:

'The principle of independent judgments (and decorrelated errors) has immediate applications for the conduct of meetings, an activity in which executives in organisations spend a great deal of their working days. A simple rule can help: before an issue is discussed, all members of the committee should be asked to write a very brief summary of their position. The procedure makes good use of the value of the diversity of knowledge and opinion in the group. The standard practice of open discussion gives too much weight to the opinions of those who speak early and assertively, causing others to line up behind them.'

The last sentence shows just how wise Kahneman is. However his suggestion that nervous, politically inclined managers would be prepared to commit their views to paper ahead of hearing what everyone else thinks about the big issue errs on the optimistic side.

My heroes Thaler and Sunstein completed their brilliant *Nudge* without mentioning meetings at all. Strange one might think, in that behavioural economics and choice architecture are custom-built to inform meetings and move discussions on.

My even greater heroes Russo and Schoemaker in *Decision Traps* didn't specifically refer to meetings, but implicitly recognised their innate weakness:

'Groups can make better decisions than individuals, but only if they are helped along by a skilful leader. There is little excuse for using costly group meetings to make inferior decisions. Unfortunately, this is what often happens'. 'Deciding how to decide is probably more important in group decisions than in individual decision-making.'

It is probably no surprise that consultants are more tuned into the meeting vibe than academics. David Taylor in *The Naked Leader* wrote:

'It seems to me that the way to master meetings is to have them sewn up before they happen, and that is more about the psychology of the individuals than the meeting itself. If you have gone to the trouble of speaking with, listening to and persuading the other attendees before the decision is taken, you will be on a firm footing for everything. How do you do this? Find out what they think/want by listening and asking questions, and make sure your solution/recommendation fits their need. Simple.' He also wrote, *'Like it or not much of our time, and energy, is spent in company meetings. We can make of these what we will – treat them as a waste of time, and this is what they will become, use them to pass the time, and that is what they will do. However, utilise them to better understand your peers and organisation and to build rapport, and the time will not be wasted; it will be an investment, with some fun thrown in as well.'*

I like the use of the word fun. Taylor knows how wearing

meetings can be, and how that gets in the way of individual performance. Fun, after all, is one of the stops on the line to joy!

Kevin Allen is a consultant, an old friend of mine, and an incorrigible and proselytising optimist. In *The Hidden Agenda* he shares much of value in a world that is very familiar to me – pitching. He also passes on some valuable advice about balancing life and work:

'I [had been] led to believe that success in business involved a mastery of cold hard facts and brutal logic. Sheer nonsense. Whether in private life or business, we are all driven by fundamental human impulses and desires. They rule our hearts.....For me the root of desire is hope.'

Kevin has provided an important reason for being determined to do something about meetings, and make them more constructive. We hate time that goes nowhere, and delivers neither value nor satisfaction. We are entitled – especially with an activity that plays such a large part in our lives – to hope for better.

The price we pay for being too busy

English business psychologist, Tony Crabbe, has written an important book. *Busy* is a comprehensive, enjoyable and persuasive tirade against ruining your life by following the false god of 'busyness'.

Busy isn't just about meetings, but a lot of the problems he identifies have been exacerbated by wall-to-wall meetings.

There follow ten warnings and ten pieces of advice, based loosely on learnings from *Busy*.

Ten warnings

1. Don't be seduced by the world of "Too much" into becoming 'crazy busy'. Crabbe warns that it is too easy to slip into a state he calls 'learned helplessness', as you start to lose control. You cannot afford to lose control over your life

2. Start and finish everything on time, as far as possible. Try and avoid being pressured into accepting unrealistic and unreasonable deadlines. Crabbe's rule of thumb is to double the timeframe someone is trying to bully you into accepting. The Planning Fallacy was the term coined by Buehler, Griffin and Ross to describe the phenomenon of people underestimating completion times

3. Don't lose the right to choose, and avoid being so tired that you have no time to think of alternatives

4. Don't allow boundaries between life and work to be compromised

5. Don't allow your career to be put on hold by 'company priorities'

6. Don't rush from meeting to meeting, unless there is absolutely no alternative. Certainly don't allow back-to-back meetings to be the norm in your life

7. Don't lose focus or momentum. Sustained focus and

attention is the opposite of busy. Busyness shows itself in the tendency to do things (lots of things) rather than focus

8. When you are working very hard – and continuously in meetings – take it seriously if your health starts to suffer

9. Or your relationships

10. Or your happiness

Ten suggestions

1. Work out what your key strengths really are and play to them. Think of the very best things you have done, and try and recapture what made that possible. A key strength – and one that attracts the right sort of attention – is making an impact, adding value, making a difference

2. Don't be embarrassed to work out what your personal brand should be – and develop it. No shame in stealing a brand and adapting it for you

3. Remember how much time you spend on autopilot – take control from time to time, and use System 2 thinking

4. 'Open the file' ahead of time. Cue in the brain the night before by thinking about the issues in your 9am meeting

5. Close the other open files (think MS Windows). Get in the zone. Focus. Don't allow yourself to be distracted

6. Give yourself plenty of recovery time. Take regular

breaks – play music, move around, change of scene, have food, have a drink, have sex!

7. Be playful sometimes. Don't be relentlessly serious. Don't be afraid to experiment

8. Just because everyone is crazy busy, it doesn't mean you have to be. 'Busy is a rubbish brand'

9. Kill at least a meeting a week. And if that works, maybe one a day, or every other day

10. Put 'stuff' in a bucket, and empty it regularly

Essentialism

Tony Crabbe suggested I also look at the work of Greg McKeown, another critic of 'Too much'. Greg has written a book called *ESSENTIALISM – The Disciplined Pursuit Of Less*. There are two of his thoughts that completely resonated with me. He reveals that when the word 'priority' first entered the English language, it was invariably used in the singular. He ridicules the very concept of having a list of ten priorities. He also recommends keeping a journal, a refreshingly old fashioned thought in the era of social media. He coined a brilliant phrase, 'the faintest pencil is better than the strongest memory'. I was reminded of it a few nights ago, when my brain was buzzing about 12.30 am, and I decided to get up and download some of the thoughts that were keeping me awake. By the next morning, and given a bit of editing, I had cracked two distinct problems that had been plaguing me for days.

McKeown has strong views on meetings:

'What if businesses eliminated meaningless meetings and replaced them with space for people to think and work on their most important projects? What if employees pushed back against time-wasting e-mail chains, purposeless projects and unproductive meetings so they could be used at their highest level of contribution to their companies and in their careers?.'

Indeed. He also tells of a friend who 'routinely skipped the weekly meeting other people attended and would simply ask them what he had missed. Thus he condensed a two hour meeting into ten minutes and invested the rest of that redeemed time getting the important work done'.

Points from Daniel Levitin's The Organized Mind

Daniel Levitin is Professor of Psychology and Behavioural Neuroscience at McGill University in Montreal. In his new book he counsels against falling for the propaganda about multi-tasking being admirable. Levitin agrees completely with Crabbe about the importance of focus. The multi-tasking tendency (Levitin calls it a 'diabolical illusion') afflicts the way people try to juggle their lives, and the ground they try to cover in meetings. He says the more we try to multi-task, the less we focus on what is important, and the more ineffective we become. 'Switching attention comes with a high cost', he says. But we all do it, particularly in meetings and from one meeting to another.

This is surely the problem with the way we do meetings

today. A diary with two meetings in the morning and two in the afternoon (not an unusual occurrence) requires us to concentrate on, say, four different subjects. Each of those meetings will probably have up to five items or aspects on the agenda. There will be somewhere between five and fifteen people in each meeting, every one of whom will have a point to make. Also we have our work to do, a situation with a family member to resolve, and the car to book in for a service. Ah yes, and we are going to go out tonight. Levitin has to be right. We weren't designed to deal with all that.

Crabbe makes a good point stressing the need to acknowledge Meeting Recovery Syndrome. Levitin tells of psychiatrists who insist on working a 50 minute hour, leaving 10 minutes between patients 'to write down what happened'.

What can get in the way of making meetings better?

Crabbe and Levitin are right. We need to take control of our lives. We know it would make sense to have the time to think better, work better and live better. It isn't only meetings standing in the way of freeing up that valuable time, but for many of us the overdose of meetings is a major contributory factor. We should all support the movement for fewer, better, more effective meetings with less people tied up in them. If time was as valuable as power sources, freeing up huge units of people's time would be the equivalent of a massive conversion to sustainable and affordable energy.

We might agree that is an example not so much of behavioural economics as a well-attested theory among business academics – the capability of analogy to influence minds and inspire meaningful change. If people are damaged, the organization is too. The advantages of more effective and productive meetings are clear:

- Companies will have directors, executives and managers who will be freed up to do more actual *work*
- Those same staff members will be able to get their lives back in balance and work better and live more happily
- And their families and friends will also benefit from this increased balance

So what's stopping us? I'll give you a couple of behavioural phenomena – Loss Aversion and Sunk Cost. Loss Aversion is the state of finding it difficult to give things up. Pundits call it FOMO (the fear of missing out). We are worried about what we might miss by not being at this meeting or that. Sunk Cost relates to the huge time investment we have made by attending hundreds of meetings. And so we feel obliged to carry on attending hundreds more. We call apologetically to explain that we can't talk because we are in a meeting. Every PA says, 'I am afraid she/he is in a meeting' several times every day. Doesn't it make sense to break free now?

We can all make a difference to meetings

Blaming our company, that other company, 'those people', even City Hall for how unproductive, sapping and pointless meetings can be is neither profitable, nor entirely fair.

There are things we can do to make our own change, and to help our colleagues. If we do have to be 'in a meeting', there are some simple things we can do to reduce the damage to ourselves and others.

Here is a quick shopping list of mistakes and meeting traps, courtesy of US blog site MeetingKing:

1. Not having a goal
Without a goal the meeting really does become purposeless. Avoid this by reviewing the meeting beforehand and understanding what you hope to achieve by going – such as sharing an update or finding out information about a project.

2. Insisting on going ahead without key people
Don't insist on pushing ahead if the people needed to provide either updates or direction are not there. The meeting will end up being aimless in that case. Instead reschedule for a time that the person or people can make it.

3. Not having reviewed the agenda
If you do not review the agenda before the meeting then you will not have a clear idea of what the meeting will be about. You will also not have prepared yourself for it effectively so there is a risk that you will be wasting other people's time at the meeting.

4. Not being prepared technically
Always make sure that the technology is in place and working in advance. Nothing is more frustrating for the

meeting attendees than you fussing around trying to get the projector to work.

5. Not checking that someone is taking minutes
If no-one is taking minutes you'll find yourself having the same meeting over again in a couple of weeks when no-one can remember what was discussed.

6. Showing up late
If you show up late the meeting may not start on time. That means you'll be wasting the time of the other participants. Turning up on time is the polite thing to do which easily gets past this problem.

7. Bringing an extra person or two with you
Unless there is a genuinely good reason for bringing the extra person, such as they are taking over from you on the project, then leave them behind.

8. Dialing in from a noisy place
On a conference call there's always one that dials in from somewhere really noisy. That makes it really hard for the rest of the attendees to be able to listen properly and concentrate. The simple solution here is – don't do it. Make sure you are prepared for your meetings properly by being somewhere quiet, or make your apologies and stay off the line.

9. Going off topic
Don't do it. It's annoying for others and it wastes their time.

It will also encourage others to do the same, meaning that your time will get wasted too. Stick to the main points of the meeting, and before you open your mouth, ask yourself, "Is this really relevant?"

10. Not raising the important questions

If you don't ask the pressing questions that concern you, maybe no one else will. Make sure that you ask for the clarity that you need so that you understand how issues affect you and so that you can do your job effectively.

◆ NOTEBITE

Meetings can be improved, but only if we keep busyness at bay, and start thinking

Chapter 5

PEOPLE CAN GO WRONG IN MEETINGS TOO

In the previous chapters we saw what a serious macro-problem time-wasting meetings have become, and how they can even be a threat to our work/life balance. It has become commonplace to blame companies and corporate governance for all these ills. We assume meetings are an entrenched problem we can do very little about. But I don't believe that is true. I think much of the hopeless inefficiency can be laid at the door of poor thinking.

Let's start with six myths

- 'The best way to kick this off is to get all the stakeholders in the room'.
- We all need to be busy, and it's perfectly okay to say, 'I'm wall to wall today'.
- 'Meetings have to be the priority in my diary'.
- 'None of us is as smart as all of us'.
- 'Don't worry about that disagreement between Stephen and Claire. One of them will persuade the other in the meeting'.
- 'I'm a great multitasker'.

Why are they myths?

- **The best way to kick this off is to get all the stakeholders in the room**

  We have already learned that having all the stakeholders in the room makes change management very difficult. It also means that we start with a lot of people in the room. Worse than that, big meetings of colleagues tend to be relentlessly internally-focused. A business lifetime of observing clients and agencies 'interrogating their brands' and 'drilling down' tells me how easy it is to forget the inconvenient threat from competition when we all have our eyes down

- **We all need to be busy, and it's perfectly OK to say, 'I'm wall to wall today'**

  There is a difference between being busy and being crazy busy. The greatest problem for business people today is being time-poor. Meetings are a significant contributor to time poverty – which is one excellent reason to do what we are attempting in this book, to fix the danger stemming from bad, unproductive meetings, for both organisations and individuals

- **Meetings are so important that they should override everything else in my calendar**

  This is a huge misapprehension, but it is one that afflicts practically every organisation in the world. *Some* meetings are very important. Others – many others – are absolutely not. There's an excellent TED talk by David

Grady on how you can get your life back by not blindly accepting every invitation *http://www.ted.com/talks/ david_grady_how_to_save_the_world_or_at_least_ yourself_from_bad_meetings?language=en*

- **None of us is as smart as all of us**
  Talk about the arrogance of the mob. This is just not true – at least in the generality. There is a classic Decision Trap – Group Failure – to explain why. Group Failure is the refusal to accept that a squad of the great and good can be wrong. And wow! How true that can be. Particularly if the group also suffer from another Trap – Confirming Evidence, whereby we believe in and agree with people who think like we do. In big meetings particularly Anchoring (being over-influenced by the first information we receive) can also be a factor. Don't forget also the famous Stanovich Theory – 'smart people can be stupid'. Also, not all opinions are equal.

- **Don't worry about that disagreement between Stephen and Claire. One of them will persuade the other in the meeting**
  Human nature being what it is, in a big meeting a disagreement between colleagues is far more likely to be made worse than bridged

- **I'm a great multitasker**
  Daniel Levitin's neurological research shows that shows that we are not wired to multi-task, in the sense of doing several things at the same time. We can certainly do

one task after another sequentially, and indeed alternate tasks and return repeatedly to one of them. But in his new book *The Organized Mind*, he counsels strongly against trying to multi-task. He explains that attempting to switch attention from one thing to another comes at a considerable cost to our focus and efficiency

◆ MOTEBITE

The moment you see lots of chairs around a table in a meeting room, take time to reflect that the meeting problem has already started.

A live example of 'persuasion' not working

The other day I was listening to Radio 5 live. Presenter Chris Warburton was doing a piece on a campaign to put newspapers on the top shelf to prevent children seeing disturbing headlines. He had recruited the standard two 'experts' – someone from a women's group who supported the idea, and a chap who thought it was ridiculous. Warburton said, "Why don't you two persuade each other to change your minds?" and predictably the two protagonists dug in behind their rehearsed (and firmly held) points of view, and gave not an inch. Was it at all surprising that neither speaker changed their mind? No. Did it make good radio? No.

Yet in meeting after meeting everyone wastes their time while people who fundamentally disagree kick seven bells out of each other. Faux democracy has much to answer for. Presumably that is the justification for giving up valuable work time for pointless debate. Confrontational and adversarial behaviour is everywhere. Why do we allow so many meetings to deteriorate into an unregulated free for all? Meetings are essentially the way we work together. So it becomes the responsibility of meeting organisers to lay down rules on behaviour and etiquette. I'm not against constructive debate. Nor do I expect everyone to turn the other cheek. But confrontational behaviour has two big downsides. Opponents seldom change their mind. And it wastes ever more valuable time.

Empathy is the miracle remedy. The next time you are gearing up for a frontal assault, just imagine yourself in the shoes of your intended target. Treat them as you would like to be treated yourself.

Big meetings are the biggest problem

Why are meetings a chore? Why do they take up too much time? Largely because there are too many people in the room. The size of meetings – the number of people around the table – is one of the biggest problems. And the miracle solutions – restricting the meeting to half an hour, making everyone stand up, building mind maps – don't help if you start with too many players. With too many people in the room, it is difficult for individuals to make much of a contribution, with so many voices wanting to be heard.

We have already looked at the Cleverness Illusion – the fallacy that a group of clever involved people will put their heads together, and come up with 'good ideas'. It doesn't work: five people, five egos. Ten people, ten egos. Fifteen people, fifteen egos. Conversation, which is the lubrication for meetings, is more difficult the more people there are who want to speak. Divide the time available for the meeting by the number of people attending and you are left with very little individual airtime. How well is that ratio of people to minutes going to work at meetings attended by bright, articulate people like you and your colleagues? Then divide the time available by the number of items likely to be on the agenda, and it's not difficult to see why there is often no time to have proper discussion of all the important issues.

The more people at a meeting, the more it will default to hierarchy. Manners and etiquette tend to suffer. Chairmanship becomes more difficult. As meeting attenders lose the chance to communicate, they lose the right to communicate. And think of the opportunity cost of five people being tied up in a 90 minute meeting. Then try that for ten people, or fifteen people! Think of all the useful things they could have been doing, and the value of what that might produce.

Let's look at the other dimensions of wasted time and money in meetings – and break down the constituent parts

We started with big meetings – too many people in the room. Now for the others:

- Too many meetings per day
- Too many meetings per person per day
- Meetings going on for too long

- Meetings being badly run and failing to deliver goals and outcomes

Sadly we find everywhere that there is a lack of process and discipline in the way meetings are organised and run. Sometimes that is down to a lack of pre-planning. Or it can be basically a lack of leadership, or too hierarchical an approach which doesn't help democracy within the team.

If an organisation, a division, a department or a team allow too many meetings to take place, both cost and opportunity cost go up, and there's bound to be more waste.

If there is no time discipline and meetings habitually overrun, or meetings are scheduled for unnecessarily long time segments, there will be even more timeburn, more cost, more opportunity cost, and more waste still.

◆ MOTEBITE

Just think of the opportunity cost of five people being tied up in a 90 minute meeting. Then try that for ten people, fifteen people! Think of all the useful things they could have been doing, and the value of what that might produce.

It is not just the fact that there are too many meetings, too many people attending, and they take too long, it's what happens at these meetings. Influential and powerful people can behave in an un-clever way. They can also behave badly! It is not uncommon to come across bad manners and behaviour. It could be over-assertiveness, or something simple like interrupting or overtalking. People don't help themselves or the organisation by behaving badly or being selfish.

Then there is passive response, for example not listening, not engaging, doing your emails, having a private conversation with your neighbour, leaving early, or simply not turning up. The consequences are just as damaging to the output, and ultimately the outcome of the meeting.

How often have we watched meetings go off-track because of highly selective provision of data and information? It is so easy for dominant personalities to bias proceedings in favour of their own ideas and suggestions.

Confrontation

Why do we play the confrontational card? Why do we behave aggressively? Why do we overtalk and interrupt? Perhaps it is a natural survival instinct in a room full of rival voices and opinions. If so, that's yet another reason to fight shy of big meetings. We all grow up to believe that meetings are helped by open discussion and constructive debate. It is a small step from there to dialectic. This is a method of argument for resolving disagreement that has been central to European and Indian philosophy since antiquity. The word originated in ancient Greece, and was made popular by Plato in the Socratic dialogues. Can it be counter-productive? Should it be discouraged in meetings? Or regulated and managed? Is debate always the best way of resolving different points of view? Is democratic discussion always a good idea?

The more I study the meeting, the more I question the value of open-ended debate. Years of overseeing 'managed meetings' in the new business process have influenced me away from free flow and towards a degree of beneficial control. But first we need to look at the characters around the table.

Major contributors to the problem are the bad boys and girls

Let me introduce you to some interesting people, all to be found around a conference table near you:

Ego

Mainly concerned with him/herself. Conceited, arrogant, self-centred and self-serving. Not collegiate. Tends to be more personality-based than behavioural.

Adverso

ADVERSO

Beyond devil's advocacy into negative behaviour, thinking and comments. This is a behavioural tendency that can turn into someone even worse...

Wrecko

WRECKO

A fully-fledged meeting wrecker. Completely counter-productive. Probably best to exclude from meetings if possible.

Domino

Dominating. Forceful. Macho. Alpha. Inclined to take meetings where he/she wants to go, even if others don't, or the direction is not in line with the meeting goal and agenda. Taking over a meeting is time-wasting as well as irritating.

Interrupto

Interrupts and overtalks continually. It is a habit many people develop to try and attract attention.

Defo

DEFO

Won't listen.

Chato

CHATO

Prone to side conversations and asides to the detriment of the flow of the meeting.

Conectado

Connected not to the meeting but to their mobile network or the internet. On one or more screens, texting, emailing.

Amigo

So friendly that he/she falls into the trap of agreeing with everything – often without being able to say why. Also capable of supporting conflicting positions.

Passivo

PASSIVO

Passive. Not engaged. Switched off. Not contributing.

Absento

ABSENTO

Missing the meeting. Not turning up.

Suppresso

Unhelpful chair/leader behaviour, not allowing people to express their views – particularly views they personally disagree with.

Cosisayso

'Here's what we must agree on'. 'This is what we are going to do'...all based on the leader's views, without much or any justification. 'Because I say so!'

I'm sure you are familiar with several of these characters. It could even be that you recognise yourself in one of them!

Here, by contrast, are some role models for better behaviour:

Constructo

Constructive, helpful, well-intentioned. An accomplished and positive debater.

Abierto

Open-minded. Good listener.

Bienvenido

The colleague who is always welcome at any meeting.
Easy personality. Charming in a good way.

Perspectivo

Not just stuck in the present. Able to view issues from both
a historical perspective, and with an eye to the future.

Summary on fallible personalities

We have all learned so much about making groups more effective from Belbin and De Bono. Belbin's work in allocating roles within the group to individuals on the basis of personality and ability rather than status was way ahead of its time. Wearing De Bono's hats – even when we were experiencing how it feels to wear the 'wrong' hat – helped us grow. It is the same principle as the Debating Society rule of being obliged to propose and second a number of motions with which you personally disagree. My typologies above are obviously about exaggerating to make a point. I profoundly believe that we all are capable of learning from getting it wrong. Defos can learn to listen, Conectados, Chatos and Interruptos can improve their behaviour. Vitally Dominos, Adversos and Passivos can realise how a more co-operative attitude can help not just the group, but also themselves. Having said that, maybe Egos and Cosisaysos will take a lot of retraining!

What else can go wrong?

Let us concentrate on the top twenty meeting problems:

Agenda stew

If the agenda is off-beam this is a pretty serious problem. Most meetings are only scheduled for 60 minutes, and quite often an agenda will have too many items to be covered in an hour. Over-stuffed agendas range from the optimistic to the absolutely unachievable. In the latter case it can have a depressing effect on the meeting, and with the wrong chairing it can mean everything being rushed, and nothing covered properly. I think sometimes people equate agendas with to do lists. It's quite all right to end a day without completing a to-do list. To start a meeting with ten items on the agenda when there's only time for three is completely irresponsible.

Arriving late

A lot of people make a habit of showing up late, and it is very disruptive, particularly in an organisation where a lot of meetings are held. If you arrive late for a train or a flight, you miss it. Meeting organisers should tell habitual late arrivals that they have missed the boat (or train or flight).

Back-to-backs

Meeting invitations fly through the air like arrows at Agincourt. Indeed there are very few restrictions on issuing them. MS Outlook has much to answer for. Organisers and participants alike need to be on the lookout for this problem. It can have a bad effect both on individuals, who need recovery time to perform well in the next meeting. It can also hamper progress, particularly in the later meetings in a day, if over-committed attendees are tired and relatively ineffective. Back-to-backs are draining enough in internal meetings. In my pitch management life there have been times when I failed to take a strong line with clients hell-bent on seeing four or even five full presentations in a day. In those circumstances the direct casualty was the exhausted client team. But the collateral damage was suffered by agencies #4 and 5, who had no way of seducing or convincing a group of catatonic marketers.

Chairing issues

Chairing meetings isn't easy. Leading a meeting is a lot more straightforward than being the chair. In my view it is something that needs training to avoid obvious errors:

- Too directive
- Too laissez-faire
- Too much of a 'Manager'
- Too much of a 'Referee'
- Too friendly to the most powerful people around the table
- Too keen to be a David Dimbleby and bring in the man in the red sweater at the back before we've heard from the panel

Donuts

UK practice with refreshments has traditionally been an interruption for coffee and biscuits to be served. In the US it is the custom to have refreshments on tap at the back or side of the room for attendees to help themselves. This is a better idea, and has recently been adopted widely here. It is much more convenient and much less disruptive. Some countries, cultures, and indeed companies, are much less generous with drinks and snacks. Indeed there are meeting gurus who are against having them available during meetings, claiming that like bathroom breaks, people should only avail themselves between sessions. For the title I'm grateful to David Pearl, whose book about meetings is called *Will there be Donuts?*

Facilities difficulties

How many hundreds of times have we seen a meeting ruined or sandbagged by a technical snafu? It is really important that companies and meeting centres have skilled technical assistance on site and ready to leap into action. If your company is not equipped, be conservative about trying anything too ambitious technically. If you are playing away, be sure to find out what facilities exist, and avoid as far as possible ill-equipped venues. In 2002 I watched a world-famous agency lose a pitch for Electrolux by passing up on an opportunity to familiarise themselves with some slightly unusual equipment in a Stockholm conference room. In the mid-1990s I learned the hard way in Nairobi that without a power surge protector, your precious slide projector could actually blow up and disintegrate. Talking of facilities, someone needs to check bathrooms, loos etc.

Goal – what goal?

You simply have to have a clear goal for every meeting. Being summoned to any meeting that doesn't have a written objective is worrying and demotivating. Even if there are impressive folk around the table, why should I spend an hour in a talking shop without a target? Also a meeting without a goal is unlikely to lead to a decision or make any real progress.

Groundhog

This is that old favourite – the meeting that is just like the last one – same place, same people, basically the same agenda. We haven't moved on. Disaster – participants will swiftly lose heart and become Passivos or even Absentos. For this title, thank you Lisa Kay Solomon.

Leaving early

A premature departure from a meeting by one or more participants is nothing like as disruptive as people arriving late. But it doesn't help. Persistent offenders should be spoken to or left out. I had a client at Ericsson in Kista who had such a poor attention span that he regularly left meetings – even ones he had called – after half an hour.

Lunchtime meeting

We call it lunchtime for a good reason. We all need regular breaks in what are inevitably long days. Fixing a meeting that stops people having at least a 30 minute break is antisocial and misguided. In case you believe it's very old school to make sure even senior executives take the breaks to which they are entitled, just look at how companies like Google and Facebook make sure their staff are well refreshed.

Missing persons

If arriving late and leaving early are significant faux pas, not turning up at all – unless there is a good reason flagged in advance –is rude, unhelpful and disrespectful to the rest of the crew. Naturally there are always going to be good reasons for non-attendance. But giving prior warning is mandatory, and then an organiser can postpone if necessary.

No follow-up

If there are minutes from last time committing individuals to take some action before the next meeting, and that action has not been forthcoming, whoever failed to deliver has let down all their colleagues, and needs to be spoken to. But this is a mutual thing. It is quite unfair simply to dump tasks on colleagues without advising them and making sure it is possible within the time specified.

Overrun

Meetings have to keep to time. Like lessons at school, the end-time of one period has to be observed if people are to get to the next one. No exceptions. My stance with clients who were relaxed about agencies overrunning was always to make sure the agency following wasn't disadvantaged by being kept waiting, and the one before didn't suffer by having significantly less time.

Pre-read famine

Most meetings go better if the participants have been provided with some background and briefing materials. They will be better prepared and it will save time. Short-changing participants is disrespectful, and will probably mean that the meeting goes less well, and achieves less.

Pre-read overload

But too much in the way of pre-reads is counter-productive. If the pre-read cannot be taken on board in the time available, it is likely that people will read none of it. In my experience of pitches, both clients and agencies are allergic to 'too much'.

Presentation pickles

'Death by Powerpoint' has become a fairly meaningless cliché. Powerpoint is still a useful tool, although there are obviously competitive software options. But meeting time is inevitably short, and it is tempting to use too many slides. It is really important to be disciplined. Equally, remember that a picture *can* be worth a thousand words.

Red herrings

From schooldays most of us appreciate the release of deviating briefly from the subject at hand into more entertaining territory. But 'briefly' is the operative word. It has to be said though that some of the most entertaining presenters and meeting participants I have met are at their most engaging when they interrupt colleagues or even themselves with stories or shafts of wit. Psychologists tell us we need to smile more. There's a TED talk by Ron Gutman, CEO of HealthTap, who claims that a single smile can stimulate the brain as much as 2,000 chocolate bars or receiving £16,000! Tony Crabbe says that only a third of adults smile more than 20 times a day.

Time mismanagement

One of the chair's principal responsibilities is not just keeping the meeting to time, but tracking progress item by item to try and ensure that as much of the agenda is covered. Keeping to time should be seen as a team responsibility as far as practicable. I know agencies that have no idea of time discipline. But they don't win many pitches

Vampired by screens

Before everyone had access to multiple portable screens, people sat in meetings looking at each other and (hopefully) taking notes. Now it can be eyes down most of the time, which severely restricts interaction. If participants are using devices to take notes or look up relevant information and data; that is of course perfectly acceptable, and a good use of technology. But doing other work in a meeting and texting or emailing outside is antisocial behaviour and poor etiquette

Venue questions

Provided there is a goal, a good agenda and the right people are present, is the venue important? The answer is that sometimes an imaginative or inspirational venue can make all the difference. In 2002 we held global pitch presentations for Cadbury in Niagara on the Lake, Ontario – a completely wonderful setting, and highly appropriate as at that time Cadbury Canada manufactured the finest Cadbury Chocolate in the world, and had a great business in that country as a result. Then in 2005 doing the agency creative briefings for Chiquita Bananas in a Brazilian restaurant in Antwerp rather than a conference room contributed to a spectacularly rich crop of agency responses.

Finally, here are a range of useful suggestions from experts and pundits to solve some of the problems above. Let's start with 8 tips from Eric Schmidt and Jonathan Rosenberg at Google (I am indebted to Kirk Vallis of Google UK for sharing these words of wisdom). Schmidt and Rosenberg say that you may have become so used to bad meetings that you accept them as a necessary evil to slog through – 'Terrible meetings plague all kinds of companies, from startups to major corporations. But a well-run meeting is something different. It's the most efficient way to present data and opinions, to debate issues, and yes, to actually make decisions.' – here are Google's rules:

Every meeting needs a leader. *A meeting between two groups of equals often doesn't result in a good outcome, because you end up compromising rather than making the best tough decisions. Designate a clear decision maker so that everyone in attendance knows who has the final word.*

The meeting needs a clear purpose and structure. A meeting that stretches on for much longer than it should most likely lacks a clearly defined purpose and structure. The *decision maker needs to call the meeting, ensure that the content is good, set the objectives, determine the participants, and share the agenda (if possible) at least 24 hours in advance. The decision maker is then responsible for summarising*

*the meeting's resolutions and email tasks to every
participant and anyone else who should be informed within
48 hours.*

**Meetings used for sharing information or brainstorming still need
owners**. *Schmidt and his team realised that if they took
a loose approach to meetings that were based on idea
dispersal or generation, what seemed like a fun session
on paper became just another waste of time. There are no
exceptions to the first two rules.*

Have a meeting only if it's necessary. *Any meeting should
have a purpose, and if that purpose isn't well defined
or if the meeting fails to achieve that purpose, maybe
the meeting should go away. If you find yourself attending
a regular meeting only of out habit, it's probably time to
redefine the meeting's purpose or else scrap it altogether.*

Don't include more than eight people. *Everyone at
a meeting should be there to give their input. Bystanders
are wasting time that could be spent being productive,
and too many eager participants lowers the quality of the
conversation. Share the results of the meeting with those
who would otherwise have been observers but could still
benefit from the information.*

Include only the necessary people, and no more. *Many times
we have walked into an 'intimate' meeting with a senior
executive from one of our customers or partners, only to
find the room full of people. They can't control what their*

customers or partners do, but they can control their own side and bring along as few people as possible. Especially for these types of important meetings, Google encourages its executives to attend only if they are needed as part of the deal, not if they are looking to feel important.

Strictly follow time constraints. Start and end on time, and leave the room at the end to summarise the discussion. If the meeting needs to run long, then incorporate appropriate time for breaks into the schedule. And if you wrap things up early, don't feel like you need to fill in the remaining time. The sooner everyone gets back to work, the better.

Be fully present in the meeting. If you take the above rules seriously, then the only meetings you'll attend are the ones you're needed in. So make sure you're actually paying attention and not sitting in a group while you catch up on email on your phone or laptop. Schmidt and Rosenberg say that this is the hardest rule to follow, and they've given up telling employees to close their laptops. *'But it's still a good rule!'* they write.

Now for some more tips

'Get into a receptive state by walking across a Thames bridge' – Clay Shirky, American internet expert

He counsels against walking into a meeting in a frenzied, preoccupied state. Crossing the Thames is clearly not the only way to clear the mind, but you get his drift.

'Hold discussions in innovative spaces....and get groups to think in new, exploratory ways' – Richard Branson

He thinks that a change of scenery and a bit of fun does wonders to encourage people to think differently.

'Hold conversations, not meetings...replace the agenda with questions' – Tony Golsby-Smith after Hans-Georg Gadamer

Don't allow your days to be filled with pointless meetings. Hold conversations instead – they are informal and creative.

'Don't just hear what co-workers or managers say. Instead actively listen' – Crystal Vogt

Listening can allow you to see problems and ideas from other perspectives.

'Hold meetings just before lunch so people will value the limited time' – Anonymous

They will also have something to immediately look forward to after the meeting.

'Look out for the Big Bad meetings, and be ready to turn them into something useful' – Lisa Kay Solomon

The Muscle Meeting – so jam-packed that participants are gasping for air.

The Military Meeting – so strictly scheduled that there's no time to do anything properly.

The Let a Thousand Flowers Bloom Meeting – no agenda, free form brainstorming.

The Groundhog Meeting – Same old, same old (see above).

'Keep asking, what problem are we trying to solve?' – Tony Crabbe

Meetings so often go off track. Essential to retain focus.

◆ MOTEBITE

Bad meetings cost a fortune, but poor behaviour and etiquette cause as many problems as bad meeting management

Chapter 6

TIME TO INTRODUCE YOU TO MOTE

> "On resiste a l'invasion des armees; on ne resiste pas a l'invasion des idees."

Victor Hugo (1802-1885), French novelist, poet, playwright and historian

(This is the origin of the famous misquote: "Nothing is more powerful than an idea whose time has come", which I hope applies to Mote!)

Every organisation could do with making meetings more productive

Meetings serve to supply our basic human need for contact and interaction. But they are also key to decision making. Each meeting should be designed to take us one or more steps along the road to a significant decision. Meetings are important to enable information, data, news, developments (whether positive or not), to be shared and disseminated. Meetings are often used to bring in expert advisers. We can also use face to face and remote meetings:

- to ask (find out information and views) – especially among stakeholders
- to persuade
- to motivate

- to negotiate
- to tell (instruct, communicate policy, decisions etc)

Managed meetings are different

Subconsciously we see meetings as free-flow. Despite the formality of conference and board rooms, meeting invitations, agendas and so forth, we still anticipate the opportunity to join in an 'improvised' event – a dinner party if you will, as opposed to a church service or a stage play. The bad boys and girls we discussed earlier play the games they do, and are able to obstruct and frustrate, precisely because the open and interactive format allows them to. The chair in a conventional meeting is essentially halfway between tour guide and referee. Even the best run 'classic' meeting cannot be described as a team effort. Note (in terms of the Super Six in chapter 2) that there is a difference between a Team Meeting – effectively a brief progress review – and a team performance with everyone on the same side.

That is exactly what a Mote is – a managed meeting on team lines.

A solution called Mote.

You might think a Mote is something in your eye – or maybe the watery surround to a more salubrious domicile. It is neither. It is my name for a new kind of meeting. It's the radical solution to a problem that vexes organisations around the world – how to have fewer meetings, and make them shorter, smaller, smarter, and dramatically more productive.

The world needs not just a better meeting; it needs something better than a meeting. Simply deconstructing and reconstructing will not do. We have to invent a new way of getting together in organisations – particularly when there are decisions to be made. To make it clear that this is a significant innovation – not a fudge – it requires its own name. I have borrowed and re-purposed a noble word from our Northern European heritage. This is the word that was used by our ancestors for gatherings to make important decisions in the community. I researched the word 'meeting' and how it translates in different languages. Mote (or Moot) was the Middle English for a meeting. Mote came into Middle English via Old English and North Saxon. Interestingly modern Swedish Möte, still use a variant of Mote to mean meeting. As with the Greeks and Romans, Mote also means the place where the meeting is held, signifying assembly or court.

Is there a scientific reason behind man's love of the meeting – over and above the obvious reasons, like dealing with crises, needing to communicate something, persuading friends and colleagues to do one thing rather than another? There are some relevant elements in Maslow's Hierarchy of Needs.

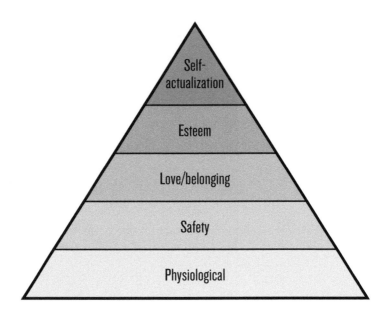

He described his fourth level of need as Esteem. Humans need to feel respected, and that they are valued by others. We can argue that holding meetings and being invited to them is very much part of this requirement for self-respect and status.

Unfortunately most companies and organisations are bedevilled by another sort of hierarchy, the pecking order, which often has precious little to do with utility or contribution. Status within a firm can easily cause problems, where the right to attend this meeting or that becomes an end in itself. It has nothing to do with attending a meeting to make a useful contribution, or to help bring about a decision. How many meetings have we attended when progress is difficult because so many of the people there are not adding value?

There is a strong argument for deconstructing the meeting, and reconstructing it as a real forum for decision making. This doesn't mean all meetings, as we said earlier. Just the ones designed to help produce a decision.

◆ MOTEBITE

The world needs not just a better meeting. It needs something better than a meeting. Simply deconstructing and reconstructing will not do.

What I'd like to tell everyone about Mote

Mote is a brand new, pioneering initiative designed to offer organisations a radical and innovative way to plan and manage better meetings. It has the potential to save huge amounts of time and money, as well as to galvanise change management and growth. It also offers individuals who are early Mote adopters a career-enhancing and life-lengthening opportunity to achieve far more in fewer meetings, regain time to do real work, and improve work/life balance.

Mote is designed specifically for *dynamic and strategic meetings* – the ones that are crucial for decision making, growth programmes, change management, driving important projects, and winning new business.

What is radical and innovative about Mote?

It is a system for holding fewer, more effective meetings,

involving less people than usual. A Mote starts small (probably maximum of 2-4 people), not with lots of occupied seats around the table. There is no Chair. The Mote is led by a **LEADER**, who manages the Mote process, sets goals, and is responsible for the output and outcomes of each Mote and the series (the deliverables). The Leader is also responsible for selling up recommendations and decisions.

The Leader is supported by his/her partner, a **NAVIGATOR**. The Navigator has to be a multi-skilled and versatile facilitator, resource investigator, timekeeper, note taker, and continuity announcer. The Navigator is responsible for setting the Motion (Mote-speak for an agenda) for each Mote and subsequent ones. If the Leader has to miss a Mote, the Navigator deputises. The Navigator is also responsible for keeping stakeholders who are not moting informed on a need to know basis.

Additional Moters are invited to join the Mote as experts and specialists. There is a problem-solving technique called Stepladder that I came across when researching *DECIDE*. Experts are called in using the Stepladder principle, which means they are let go when they have made their contribution. A Mote can also accommodate Remoters – contributors joining the Mote externally via telecon and video.

A good Mote will develop from Moters having a break before and afterwards. Back-to-backs tend to make it easy to recall the benefits of meeting number one, and difficult to get a flying start in number two. Each Mote has a Motion (like an agenda but shorter), a goal and hopefully a deliverable.

The essentials of the dynamic Mote meeting system

It is never just one meeting. It is always a series of Motes. It is a journey towards making a big decision or bringing a project to fruition. As Stephen Kneeland (author of *Effective Problem Solving*) puts it, it is about 'bridging the gap between the way things are and the way they ought to be'.

Success is based on effectively trained Leaders and Navigators, and dedicated Moters and Remoters. The aim is to start lean, leveraging the extraordinary power of two people to move projects forward and adding experts, specialists and stakeholders one person at a time, before letting them go when they have made their contribution.

It is vital that everyone is kept involved and up to speed, especially those who aren't invited to every Mote. Then the process finishes lean, moving speedily and efficiently towards executing the decision and realising the project. The crucial meeting skills deployed are planning, managing, participating, writing up and following through.

What is involved in a Mote

Let's say I am calling the Mote. I have a very clear agenda, and I become the Leader. I know exactly what kind of decision we need. Having organised my thoughts, facts and figures and aims, I involve one other person – you for example. You become the Navigator, and we conduct an informal Pre-Mote, where I take you through my thinking, goal, problems, opportunities and bring you up to date with where I have got to. This brings you into the discussion, and because it's a one-to-one – the easiest and most productive set-up – we'll probably make excellent progress.

There are essential planning steps to ensure a successful series of Motes (described in detail later in the book), and in particular a productive first session for which we will need a date, a room and an initial cast-list. Everyone will be invited and sent an outline brief.

Once we have launched the Mote we will need a third and possibly a fourth Moter. These might be colleagues to bounce ideas off. Or we might need to bring to bear some specialist expertise or experience. We always re-start the same way after a new Moter is introduced: recap, summarise, tell the newcomers what help we need from them.

This will not go on indefinitely. Using Stepladder, and only going up one player at a time, you'll find you seldom get past 5 or 6 people at the Mote. And this is a major eye-opener, considering how many participants the average meeting *starts* with. It is a really efficient way of working.

By using Stepladder in the early stages of a Mote, we take advantage of a number of psychological factors. The most effective of all human interactions is the one-to-one encounter. A Mote that starts with just the Leader and Navigator is bound to make fast, early progress. From the Pre-Mote we have our overall goal clearly in focus, and also the brief for the decision we need. The Pre-Mote will also have clarified the main problems (and hopefully solved them) and focused on the most important opportunities. With inputs like this the Leader and Navigator can probably achieve more in the first hour of a Mote than most fully-staffed conventional meetings can manage in three. It will be obvious to both the first two players when additional inputs are needed, and then the new Moters can be brought in one by one, briefed and asked to contribute.

The other people joining a Mote are not participants, or delegates. And they are most certainly not time-servers or cannon fodder. They are vitally important members of the decision making team. We always refer to them as Moters.

It's a bit like the theatre or a sports team, where the audience/fans see a team performance, but the team only works because each player has been specifically cast and given a named part or position.

Learnings from Belbin

Meredith Belbin was the pioneer of team roles. Still alive and active in his late eighties, Belbin published a seminal book, *Management Teams*, in 1981. He gave the world nine typologies (originally seven), each one constituting a key team role:

- Plant: the left field problem-solver
- Resource Investigator: networker who recruits outside expertise, so reducing the group's dependence on received wisdom
- Monitor-Evaluator: the devil's advocate and objective stickler
- Completer Finisher: detail zealot

- Shaper: rigorous visionary who can guide the group under pressure
- Co-ordinator: the one who insists on everyone being consulted and listened to
- Team Worker: HR person
- Implementer: tasked with finding workable solutions and implementation
- Specialist: expert in whatever discipline is needed

Casting for a Mote needs to be on the basis of function, rank, expertise, and responsibility as well as Belbin's roles.

But in Motes we don't need teams of nine, so there will be choices to make, and a degree of doubling up. The Leader is clearly going to be Shaper and Implementer, while the Navigator will combine the roles of Co-ordinator, Resource Investigator and Completer Finisher. This leaves us to find Plant and Monitor-Evaluator from among the Moters, while looking to Stepladder to bring on board the required Team Workers and Specialists as we need them.

The Belbin Team Roles Model can be used before a project starts to maximise balance. As the Mote series develops, Leader and Navigator can observe the individual members of the team, and see how they behave and contribute. The Belbin approach can help inform whether one or more team members could improve how they work together and with others to avoid potential conflict of their natural styles. It is also useful to establish whether new skills need to be brought onto the team to cover weaknesses.

Yet it's only one factor, however powerful. Belbin's insight about the need for a balanced make-up has been crucial in the search for effective problem solving and decision making. We owe him a great deal.

What does a Mote look like?

A Mote is diamond-shaped, or more accurately like a pyramid on top of an inverted pyramid.

The shape symbolises both the balance between the initial, middle and final stages, and the likely number of players. The Mote starts small with the Leader and Navigator, and as the decision comes to be finalised a small group will again work best. During the exploration of options, the reward/risk analysis, and discussion of possible solutions, more expertise will be brought to bear.

We already have our goal, because we set it in advance, expressing what the Mote is designed to achieve. This effectively defines the agenda as there is no room for other items, any other business etc. The English word agenda comes from the Latin – what has to be done. But we use Motion in a Mote, to stress the degree of focus that is needed. A Mote is driven by what has to be achieved, most often a decision. You don't need the minutes of the last meeting. You don't need a shopping list of 12-20 items that have to be discussed. You need a simple Motion that focuses precisely on why everyone is there, and what they have to decide upon.

Almost certainly a Mote will consist of more than one session, because Decision Making, Change Management and Problem Solving are all journeys. Individual sessions are likely to have different participants, with, as we have seen, few players at the beginning and end of the process, and more in the middle.

Motes can take place anywhere, but it can help underline the importance of a Mote if it does take place in a special or relevant location. This might involve going to a particularly appropriate city or country, where geographical, political or cultural influences might add to the impact. The venue itself must be comfortable, well-appointed, and equipped with all necessary technology, including facilities for importing contributions from remote participants (Remoters).

How does the Mote help us reach and produce a decision? The key is to look at the options we identified at Pre-Mote stage. To qualify, each of the options has to be a valid way forward. We start by looking at the upsides and downsides of each option, and in particular the most attractive upside, and the most worrying downside in each case. Levitin in *The Organized Mind* advocates what he calls 'Planning for Failure' – thinking about anything that can possibly go wrong to ensure that every downside has been anticipated, with a ready-made course of action in hand.

Then we carry out a reward/risk analysis in each case.

The most attractive option is almost certainly going to be the one with the most positive upside, consistent with not having potentially disastrous consequences.

Will this necessarily be the decision we are going to make? All the evidence from the neuroscientists tells us that our emotions and instincts are as important as our rationality. We need to feel comfortable with our decision, as well be able to justify it logically. Traditional methods like sleeping on it are as valid as ever. Then we need to do something that sounds painfully obvious (but you'd be amazed how often it is not done properly) – write the Decision down, precisely and accurately. That is the job of the Navigator. It can't be delegated, although obviously Moters can be asked to help.

The core principles of Mote

There are five:

- **GAME PLAN**
- **SMALL AGILE TEAM**
- **STEPLADDER**
- **PERFORMANCE**
- **SPIRIT OF MOTE**

First is the **Game Plan** – a hand-picked Leader and Navigator managing a series of meetings to achieve a specific and usually ambitious goal. Each session needs to be meticulously planned. The Leader is the driver of growth and change. Fortunately Leader candidates are easy to identify by role and personality, although they need training to maximise the effectiveness of the Mote. The Leader is not a Chairperson, because a Mote is not an Assembly Meeting. The Leader should also be in charge of the Spirit of Mote

The Navigator role is crucial, both as a Monitor Evaluator and Resource Investigator. This is the key innovation, and Navigators also need specialist training. Navigators are likely to come from planning or ops. It is vital to recruit people particularly suited to being meeting specialists. Navigator represents a genuine career development opportunity.

The second principle is that the Mote is essentially a **Small Agile Team**, quite unlike the big meetings packed with mavericks pursuing their own agenda that bedevil processes in many companies. First and foremost it is a team of hand-picked Moters, with balanced personalities and roles, tasked to *think together* and *work together*. It is a similar situation to sport, the theatre or music. Not everyone will be a good Moter, but it requires serious professionals who are involved for what they can contribute, not their status or job title. They will be dedicated to high levels of meeting performance and to helping colleagues achieve the same.

The third principle – also designed to keep Motes lean and fit – is **Stepladder**, the process of adding only one Moter at a time (or remoters dialling in) and letting people go when they have made their contribution. It is vital to include talent who can't be physically present, without disrupting those who are. Stepladder was a problem-solving technique, now largely forgotten, from many years ago. It has a key part to play in the world of Mote.

The fourth principle is **Performance**, as in driving projects, managing change, and making decisions. Motes are dedicated to outputs and outcomes. We use short and focused Motions, not long agendas. The inflection point is critical, moving from inputs to outputs, accelerating the project, bringing change that bit nearer, and making the decision. It is crucial to keep stakeholders informed and involved through excellent communications, reporting progress regularly, and letting everyone know how far the Mote has travelled towards its goal. This ensures that the Mote is efficient and productive. Finally the Mote is wrapped up and the planning starts on the next one.

The fifth and final principle is **Spirit of Mote**, the philosophy which folds in empathy and overtly collaborative behaviour to avoid debate becoming adversarial and counter-productive. Emotional intelligence is very important for good meetings. The Spirit of Mote is a team ethic. Spirit of Mote can be very effective in **all** meetings (not just Motes), and in the workplace at large.

Let's return immediatly to the fourth principle, Performance, to see how it is impacted by Spirit of Mote. Performance in a Mote is delivered in three modes:

Thinking together
Working together
Succeeding or Winning together.

Thinking together is the innovation, compared to an ordinary meeting. We tend to regard thinking as a solitary activity and working as something which is very often collaborative. It is not like that in a Mote. Empathy and collaborative behaviour mean that Moters are empowered to literally and figuratively put their heads together to think, strategise, analyse, solve problems and identify opportunities.

So **Working together** is not necessarily the start point. Moters don't tend to start working together until the inflection point has been reached – the moment when the group feels ready to move from gathering and assimilating inputs to generating outputs.

Succeeding or Winning together is the process of preparing to take the achievement of the meeting out of the conference room into the outside world.

Mote is the answer for dynamic meetings

Mote has been designed for 'dynamic meetings' –change management, big projects, and decision making. It is a head and heart solution. It is a system to manage however many meetings it takes to make a decision, manage a change, or turbocharge a project. But it is also an emotional and people solution to the meeting nightmare.

So a Mote is essentially a turbocharged meeting dedicated to driving a project or making a decision. I term these meetings 'dynamic' or 'strategic'. Change management and decision making receive the importance they deserve by holding Motes, and leaving the word 'meeting' to refer to other kinds of meeting.

The Mote is effective because it helps people co-operate more readily, and work together better in all types of meetings and in business in general. Mote is the moment we understand that a meeting can be compact, cast, produced, and perfected, and we will never willingly go back to big meetings, where people behave badly, and seldom achieve.

Mote is an ancient word and was certainly not designed as an acronym. But lovers of mnemonics might care to remember Mote like this:

Method (Game Plan. Leader and Navigator. Stepladder)
Outcome (A meeting entirely geared to outcomes and deliverables – not people, inputs and discussion)
Time (Designed to save time and cost)
Empathy (Built around collaborative behaviour)

◆ MOTEBITE
Remember the Five Principles of Mote:

→ Gameplan

→ Small AgileTeam

→ Stepladder

→ Performance

→ Spirit

Chapter 7

A VERY LITTLE KEY WILL OPEN A VERY HEAVY DOOR

Charles Dickens, *Hunted Down*

The Spirit of Mote

Mote is not just a new way of working, or a better meeting system for dynamic meetings. It is also an attitude, an approach, and a way of behaving. The Spirit of Mote is grounded in empathy, and closely based on the Golden Rule (see below). The philosophy of Mote can work for all meetings and be beneficial throughout the workplace. Correcting the negative and counter-productive influence of bad meeting culture is a huge task – a heavy door indeed. Empathy may sound like a very little key, but bear with me.

The Golden Rule

Christianity, Judaism, Hinduism, Islam, Confucianism, Jainism and Buddhism, as well as many other world religions, recognise the 'ethic of reciprocity' as a central tenet. As it says in Matthew 7.12, 'Whatever you wish that men would do to you, do so to them'.

The Golden Rule underpins the philosophy of Mote, and gives us what we call the Spirit of Mote.

President Barack Obama and the Spirit of Mote

Extract from the State of the Union Address, January 2015

'So I know the good, and optimistic, and big-hearted generosity of the American people who, every day, live the idea that we are our brother's keeper, and our sister's keeper. And I know they expect those of us who serve here to set a better example. So the question for those of us here tonight is how we, all of us, can better reflect America's hopes. I've served in Congress with many of you. I know many of you well. There are a lot of good people here, on both sides of the aisle.

And many of you have told me that this isn't what you signed up for -- arguing past each other on cable shows, the constant fundraising, always looking over your shoulder at how the base will react to every decision.

Imagine if we broke out of these tired old patterns. Imagine if we did something different.

Understand, a better politics isn't one where Democrats abandon their agenda or Republicans simply embrace mine; a better politics is one where we appeal to each other's basic decency instead of our basest fears. A better politics is one where we debate without demonizing each other, where we talk issues and values and principles and facts, rather than "gotcha" moments or trivial gaffes or fake controversies that have nothing to do with people's daily lives.'

Mote is a good idea because:

1. It is a professional, dedicated meeting system
   - To help organisations function faster and more efficiently
   - Executives and managers get more out of meetings
   - Creating more meeting down time so they have more time to think, plan and do their work
   - Motes are the meetings clever people want to go to

2. Things progress faster:
   - Fewer meetings – so that each meeting becomes more special and significant
   - Smaller meetings – tying down less key people, and giving more airtime to the people who are there
   - Tight agendas (Motions)
   - Avoiding back-to-backs
   - More effective meetings
   - More dynamic meetings

3. It is designed particularly for:
   - Decision making
   - Projects
   - Innovation
   - Transformations and change management

4. Key Players:
   - The 'Dynamic Duo' – Leader and Navigator
   - Moters (introduced on the Stepladder system), including a reporter

- Specialists and experts

5. Best information in and out:
   - IT
   - Technology
   - No need to use meetings to catch up
   - Reduce FOMO
   - Insist on pre-reads and post-meeting action summaries being read

◆ MOTEBITE

Motes are the meetings clever people want to go to

Spirit of Mote is a good idea because:

- It promotes best behaviour
- Empathy
- Agreeableness
- Discipline
- Good meeting etiquette
- Team members chosen for the contribution they make, not their job titles
- Constructive debate
- Not adversarial
- No room for egos and needless devil's advocacy
- Creativity and innovation encouraged
- Tight format
- Use of unconventional / stimulating venues

- Minimise use of remoters, unless it is essential. People not at the meeting can contribute remotely and be informed afterwards
- Positive HR implications
- Recruitment – pathfinders not mavericks
- Constructive use of graduates and interns
- Development of professional meeting specialists
- Systematic use of profiling in team building
- Training and guidelines for all Mote attenders
- Coaching
- Accountability on the way executives operate, work, contribute to company goals
- Retrain Leaders to reduce Suppresso and Cosisayso tendencies
- Retrain Egos and Dominos to be more empathic
- Retrain Adversos to be more empathic, constructive, open and flexible
- Retrain Pasivos to encourage them to join in and contribute
- Retrain Interruptos, Chatos, Conectados, Defos, Amigos and Absentos
- The Mote potential
- The best of Mote (empathy and better behaviour) can be used in ALL meetings – and in the workplace as a whole

Mote will deliver beyond making meetings better, because it is a philosophy, not just a system.

Mote is a system to manage however many meetings it takes to make a decision, manage a change, or turbocharge a project. It is also an emotional and people-led solution to the meeting nightmare.

It is a head and heart solution. It will help people co-operate more readily, and work better together in all types of meetings and in business in general. Every time I expose Mote to people, they can see that it is far more than just a better approach to managing meetings.

It is a *philosophy*. It is a way of behaving, a differentiating way of doing business, a more civilised and constructive way. The core reason that Mote works in meetings is because it allows clever, dynamic people to be positive, creative and inventive – as opposed to egotistical and point-scoring. Mote allows everyone to flourish because it gives priority to those individual Moters with the skills that are required – no those who are higher in a hierarchy or can shout the loudest!

Look at the distinctive characteristics of Mote in the meeting context:

- Positive behaviour and language
- Emphasis on etiquette – only one person speaking at a time, and avoiding the use of devices except to look things up or take notes
- Fewer meetings
- Smaller meetings
- More productive meetings
- Agenda driven by individual ideas
- The Leader role

- The Navigator role
- The Recorder role
- The 'dynamic duo' factor
- Always starting small not big
- Concentrating on the people there, not the 'remoters' dialling in
- Planned, not largely spontaneous

Mote may be an old word for meeting and meeting place. But it is also a new word to signify a streamlined meeting system, with the promise of liberating business from the broken, atrophied world of meetings with which we are so familiar.

◆ MOTEBITE
Mote is a head and heart solution

It is this new word that I want to take further to mean not just a co-operative way of working, but a positive philosophy:

- Mote principles
- Mote values
- Mote ethos
- Mote style
- Mote behaviour
- Mote language
- Mote discipline
- Mote teamwork

- Mote attitude
- Mote thinking
- The Mote way
- Inner Mote

We are talking about body language (friendliness, smiles), word language (discussion vs arguing, agreeing vs contesting) and attitude (co-operative, open). Mote is not a 'selfie' world. It's unselfish and collaborative. It's a philosophy that encourages constructive debate and brainstorming, but always with half-an-eye to taking advantage of the knowledge personality profiling gives us.

Armed with this much more broad-based vision of Mote, we can take not just the concept but the reality into all kinds of meetings. Furthermore it can reach beyond the world of meetings into life at work in general. Mote principles will work admirably in chemistry meetings, in briefing meetings, in tissue sessions, in pitching; and consider the positives of a Mote approach to problem solving, and the identification and realisation of opportunities! This is Mote thinking and Mote framing.

Mote can offer a powerful HR dimension in recruitment, but way beyond that in terms of enhancing and combining talents, and having the right people in every room. Motes are indeed super meetings, but the beneficial effects of the philosophy have the capacity to extend far beyond the conference room into almost every aspect of life in the organisation.

◆ MOTEBITE

'Have a heart that never hardens, and a temper that never tires, and a touch that never hurts'

Charles Dickens, *Hard Times*

Why does Mote work? Because people are ready to work in a more co-operative way, avoiding the pitfalls and excesses of existing meeting processes and meeting behaviour.

A new book *Empathy – A handbook for revolution* has recently been published by a British philosopher called Roman Krznaric (Ebury/Random House 2014). The book is mainly about the very ambitious goals that can be achieved by being altruistic and putting oneself in the shoes of others. It was fascinating to me that Krznaric (like Levitin, who is also a musician and a former record producer) is another polymath. He brackets his role as a proselytising philosopher with being one of the finest exponents in the UK of the ancient game of Real Tennis.

Neuroscientists have even identified the precise part of the brain (the right supramarginal gyrus) that controls our empathic responses and autocorrects if we haven't identified sufficiently with the feelings and needs of others.

Instinctively I knew how destructive bad meeting behaviour can be. Before I read Krznaric's book I never suspected that we are actually hard-wired to be considerate. We can have great Leaders and Navigators. We can use Stepladder to keep Motes lean and fit for purpose. But if people try to dominate, overtalk, interrupt, become adversarial or sulk, no progress is going to be made.

It is important to encourage this 'better behaviour' in meetings, which I have felt all along is an essential part of Mote. I borrowed the old phrase 'Party Manners' for this as an appeal to people's better natures. It is about emotional intelligence. It also relates to discovering what you share with other people, rather than concentrating on what you don't.

Roman Krznaric – Six habits of highly empathic people:

- Switch on your empathic brain – train ourselves to get better at it. Be curious
- Make the imaginative leap – brave it into other people's worlds, and try to empathise with people whose beliefs we don't necessarily share. 'Walk a mile in another man's moccasins before you criticise him'. Discover commonalities
- Seek experiential adventures – stop talking and start doing
- Practise the craft of conversation – penetrate the darkness in other people by talking to them, and 'listen hard'
- Travel in your armchair – imagine the worlds that live outside our everyday lives
- Inspire a revolution – use empathy to change the world

Peter Mead – **When in Doubt Be Nice**

An advertising legend, Peter Mead, founder of AMV BBDO, the UK's number one agency for over 20 years, has just published *When in Doubt Be Nice*. This is another plea for civilised behaviour in the business world. Mead has six tips for creating a civilised workplace:

i.   Have a firm set of principles and beliefs
ii. Make profit a consequence and not a principle
iii. Don't make staff anxious about their jobs – just concerned that the company should succeed
iv. Never allow complacency
v.   Hire well and take responsibility for your people
vi. When in doubt be nice

Alan H Palmer – **Talk Lean**

Probably the best book about meetings in recent times has been written by Alan H Palmer. It's entitled *Talk Lean*, and I return to it in Chapter 12. Palmer's core philosophy is politeness and clarity. He asks, 'If someone...approaches you for something or to tell you something, how do you want things to be said, how do you like the other person to speak to you?'

He summarises the answers he always gets in two columns, as below:

Content	Manner
Clear	Polite
Direct	Calm
Straight to the point	Respectful
Simple	Courteous
Precise	Warm
Concise	Humour (if possible)
Concrete	

The spirit of Mote will work anywhere

Beyond the Mote itself, where constructive behaviour and positive attitude is baked in to a lean and agile process to ensure dynamic progress, I firmly believe that all other types of meeting (assembly, briefing, team, learning and selling) will benefit from civilised and good-humoured behaviour, a culture of empathy, and Party Manners – politeness, in other words. It is in the wider workplace where the real benefits will accrue. That for me is the strongest response to any possible worries about the emphasis on empathy being a sign of weakness.

Why would people be prepared to change the way they behave in meetings? Is it mainly altruism? No, actually self-interest is the main reason. We feel good when we do good. We are also well regarded when we do good, so it can be a route to personal advancement (the bosses approve!). Peer pressure and encouragement is another factor. Enlightened self-interest and altruism can come together here, to the benefit of others, the team and the meeting.

Fundamental techniques in handling people

- Criticism is futile because it puts a person on the defensive and usually makes him strive to justify himself.
- Criticism is dangerous, because it wounds a person's pride, hurts his sense of importance (everyone wants to feel important/wanted) and arouses resentment.
- Instead of condemning everyone, try to figure out why they are how they are – 'To know all is to forgive all'.
- 'I will speak ill of no man... and speak all the good I know of everybody'.
- Many great leaders stood out because of this principle. Men like Abraham Lincoln made it a point at some point in his life to never criticise anyone.
- Don't criticise, condemn, or complain.

The big secret of dealing with people

- There is only one way to make someone do something, which is making them want to do it.
- The deepest craving in human nature is the craving to be appreciated.
- The best way to develop the best that is in a person is through appreciation and encouragement – Charles Schwab.
- Be anxious to praise and loath to find fault.
- 'Once I did bad and that I heard ever/Twice I did good, but that I heard never'.
- Let others know you appreciate them or something about them often.

- There is a major difference between appreciation and flattery.
- Don't just tell someone something small like 'You're doing great' or 'Looking good!', but tell them HOW they're doing great.
- Tell others you appreciated something they did.
- Give honest and sincere appreciation.

He who can do this holds the whole world with him. He who cannot walks a lonely way

- Think about things from other people's perspective.
- Put the other person's wants before your own.
- Convince this person of how something can benefit them.
- Arouse in the other person an eager want.
- Arouse in the other person an eager want.

Do this and you'll be welcome anywhere

- You can make more friends in 2 months by becoming genuinely interested in other people than you can in two years trying to get people interested in you.
- We like people whom admire us.
- 'We are interested in others when they are interested in us' – Publilius Syrus.
- Greet people with animation and enthusiasm.
- Say Hello to people in a way that shows you are pleased to talk with them.
- Become genuinely interested in other people.

A simple way to make a good impression

- Actions speak louder than words. A smile says 'I like you. You make me happy. I am glad to see you'.
- Smile, don't give an insincere grin. Insincere grins are mechanical and resented. Give real, heartwarming smiles that uplift the room.
- Smile even when on the phone. Your smile will come through the phone through your voice.
- You must have a good time meeting people if you expect them to have a good time meeting you.
- If you don't feel like smiling, force yourself to smile. Act as if you were already happy, and that will tend to actually make you happy. Psychologist William James – 'Action seems to follow feeling, but really action and feeling go together.... Thus the sovereign voluntary path to cheerfulness... is to sit up cheerfully and to act and speak as if cheerfulness was already there....
- Your mental attitude determines your happiness. 'There is nothing either good or bad, but thinking makes it so' – Shakespeare.
- To someone who has seen a dozen people scowl, frown, or turn away their faces, your smile will be like the sun breaking through the clouds.
- Smile.

If you don't do this, you are headed for trouble

- People value their name or whatever nickname it is that they go by.

- Remember people's names. Make an effort to remember their names the first try. Don't even spell the name wrong if you can.
- Remember that a person's name is to that person the sweetest and most important sound in any language.

An easy way to become a good conversationalist

- If you want to be a good conversationalist, be an attentive listener. To be interesting, be interested. Ask questions that people will enjoy answering. Encourage them to talk about themselves and their accomplishments.
- Be a good listener. Encourage others to talk about themselves.

How to interest people

- The royal road to a person's heart is to talk about things he or she treasures most.
- Try and focus on what that person is interested in and talk about it. Franklin Roosevelt, before having a visitor in his office, used to study topics he knew his guest would be interested in discussing before they came over.
- Talk in terms of the other person's interests.

How to make people like you instantly

- Always make the other person feel important.
- 'Do unto others as you would have others do unto

you'. If you want to be appreciated, feel important, worthwhile, give that feeling to others first.

- Make the other person feel important – and do it sincerely.

You can't win an argument

- Avoid arguments like you would rattlesnakes or earthquakes. Most of the time, they'll just make someone feel embarrassed, uncomfortable, or hurt their pride and make them feel inferior to you.

- There was a truck salesman who wouldn't sell many trucks because he would argue a lot with customers who would complain or make remarks about the trucks he would sell. After he had been advised to stop arguing, the salesman became one of the best salesmen his company had ever seen. If someone said something like 'I don't want a white truck! I'm going to go buy _____ truck from (random company)'. The truck salesman could agree with the salesman that the competitor's truck was indeed a good truck, and speak of its quality. THEN, he would go back and speak about the quality of the white truck he was trying to sell.

- A misunderstanding is never ended by an argument but by tact, diplomacy, conciliation and a sympathetic desire to see the other person's viewpoint.

- If someone tries to argue with you and brings up a point you haven't thought of, show them appreciation of that point and talk on that.

- Don't trust your first instinct when you feel an argument coming up. Sometimes we react harshly when we feel we have to defend ourselves or a certain point. Sometimes it brings out the worst in us.
- Control your temper.
- Listen First. Give them a chance to talk and try to find understandings.
- Look for areas of agreement.
- Apologise for mistakes or errors you've made while arguing. Pride aside.
- Promise to think over your opponents' ideas and study them carefully, and mean it. Your opponent could be right, and it's better you check it out and learn then them say 'I tried to tell you, but you wouldn't listen'.
- Thank your opponents for their interest in what you were discussing and them wanting to improve upon what you believe.
- Perhaps postpone a debate/argument for a day so that you both can get your head clear and gather facts together. Gives you both more time to think through each other's points and whether the argument is worth your friend's pride or not. What might you lose if you win the argument?
- The only way to get the best of an argument is to avoid it.

These pearls of wisdom were penned in 1936. Dale Carnegie's *How to Win Friends and Influence People* sold 15 million copies and changed a lot of lives. I think I was still at university when I read it, and it made a deep impression on a headstrong young man who thought he knew it all. I wouldn't say I became one of Carnegie's star disciples, but the book definitely saved me from some of my worst excesses. As counsel for people trying to make meetings work better it takes some beating. I am grateful to Sam Lloyd and his blogsite for providing such a good summary of Carnegie's message, of which the passage above is an extract.

◆ MOTEBITE

Don't trust your first instinct when you feel an argument coming up. Sometimes we react harshly when we feel we have to defend ourselves or a certain point. Sometimes it brings out the worst in us.

The Psychology of Mote

I looked at the 'Big Five' personality traits in psychology (the 'OCEAN' system): Openness, Conscientiousness, Extraversion, Agreeableness and Neuroticism.

OCEAN is probably more relevant to a group activity like a meeting than familiar personality profiling techniques like Myers Briggs or DISC, which are designed to assess individuals. The OCEAN traits apply to men and women individually, but they also work well in a group context. Of the five traits, I would pick out Agreeableness as the keystone of Mote behaviour. Conscientiousness is an important ingredient, with Neuroticism the polar opposite. Openness is an exciting and creative element, but potentially controversial; similarly Extraversion. Here is some more background to the Big Five:

Agreeableness – IDEAL FOR MOTE

A personality trait manifesting itself in individual behavioural characteristics that are perceived as kind, sympathetic, cooperative, warm and considerate. Agreeableness reflects individual differences in *cooperation* and social harmony. People who score high on this dimension tend to believe that most people are honest, decent, and trustworthy.

There are five subsets of Agreeableness:

- *Forgiveness*: A measure of an individual's response to deception or other transgressions. Individuals who score high on this facet tend to regain their trust and re-establish friendly relations by forgiving the offender.
- *Gentleness*: A measure of how an individual typically evaluates others. Individuals who score high on this facet tend to avoid being overly judgmental.
- *Flexibility*: A measure of behaviours related to compromise and cooperation. Individuals who score high on this facet prefer cooperation and compromise as means of resolving disagreement, while those who score low tend to be stubborn, argumentative, and unwilling to accommodate others.
- *Patience*: A measure of one's response to anger and

aggravation. Individuals who score high on this facet tend to be able to tolerate very high levels of anger and maintain their composure while expressing anger. Those who score low on Patience have difficulties remaining calm while expressing their anger and tend to have quick tempers, becoming very angry in response to comparatively little provocation.

• *Altruism:* The opposite of *Antagonism*. This facet assesses the extent to which an individual is sympathetic, soft-hearted, and helpful.

Agreeable individuals value getting along with others. They are generally considerate, kind, generous, trusting and trustworthy, helpful, and willing to compromise their interests with others. Agreeable people also have an optimistic view of human nature. Because agreeableness is a social trait, research has shown that one's agreeableness positively correlates with the quality of relationships with one's team members. Agreeableness also positively predicts *transformational leadership* skills. In a study conducted among 169 participants in leadership positions from a variety of professions, individuals were asked to take a personality test and have two evaluations completed by directly supervised subordinates. Leaders with high levels of agreeableness were more likely to be considered transformational rather than *transactional*:

• I am interested in people.
• I sympathise with others' feelings.
• I have a soft heart.

- I take time out for others.
- I feel others' emotions.
- I make people feel at ease.

Conscientiousness

A tendency to show self-discipline, act dutifully, and aim for achievement against measures or outside expectations. It is related to the way in which people control, regulate, and direct their impulses. High scores on conscientiousness indicate a preference for planned rather than spontaneous behavior. The average level of conscientiousness rises among young adults and then declines among older adults.

- I am always prepared.
- I pay attention to details.
- I get chores done right away.
- I like order.
- I follow a schedule.
- I am exacting in my work.

This is good for Mote, more in terms of contribution than behaviour.

Openness

People who are open to experience are intellectually curious, open to emotion, sensitive to beauty and willing to try new things. They tend to be, when compared to closed people, more creative and more aware of their feelings. They are also more likely to hold unconventional beliefs.

- I have a rich vocabulary.
- I have a vivid imagination.
- I have excellent ideas.
- I am quick to understand things.
- I use difficult words.
- I spend time reflecting on things.
- I am full of ideas.

This can be positive for Mote – but shouldn't be allowed to dominate.

Extroversion

Above average engagement with the external world. Extroverts enjoy interacting with people, and exhibit lots of energy. They tend to be enthusiastic, action-oriented individuals. They are highly visible in the group, like to talk and assert themselves.

- I am the life and soul of the party.
- I don't mind being the center of attention.
- I feel comfortable around people.
- I start conversations.
- I talk to a lot of different people at parties.
  This is wrong for mote.

Neuroticism

The tendency to experience negative emotions, such as anger, anxiety, or depression. It is sometimes called emotional instability. According to Eysenck's (1967) theory of personality, neuroticism is interlinked with low tolerance for stress or aversive stimuli. Those who score high in neuroticism are emotionally reactive and vulnerable to stress. They are more likely to interpret ordinary situations as threatening, and minor frustrations as hopelessly difficult. Their negative emotional reactions tend to persist for unusually long periods of time, which means they are often in a bad mood. For instance, neuroticism is connected to a pessimistic approach toward work, confidence that work impedes personal relationships, and apparent anxiety linked with work. These problems in emotional regulation can diminish the ability of a person scoring high on neuroticism to think clearly, make decisions, and cope effectively with stress.

- I am easily disturbed
- I change my mood a lot.
- I get irritated easily.
- I get stressed out easily.
- I get upset easily.
- I have frequent mood swings.
- I often feel blue.
- I worry about things.

Gyro research – what motivates business leaders to take decisions and what they worry about

I have always been a curious person. I have sat through a quarter of a century of client/agency sessions during numerous pitch processes, and wondered why clients and other people's agencies are so much nicer to each other than the contracted (ie 'married') clients and agencies I remember so well from my 20 years working in agencies.

Over my whole career I have been struck by the way business leaders make decisions. Until I did the research and interviews for *DECIDE* I thought it was just me that had noticed that senior decision makers were often more mindful of the context in which a decision is taken than the substance and issues of the decision itself. Then the Gyro agency, which specialises in business-to-business were kind enough to share with me some fascinating research they have recently conducted in both the US and UK.

In the US, Gyro, in co-operation with the Fortune Knowledge Group discovered in a survey of more than 700 high-level executives that leaders tend to make decisions emotionally, then justify them rationally. 62% of executives rely on gut feelings and soft factors. Some other findings:

- 65% believe subjective factors that can't be quantified (including company culture and corporate values) make a difference when evaluating proposals. Having sat through countless procurement –driven processes, when decisions were supposed to be made on multivariate criteria, I can only agree. 'Liked that lot, didn't like the other lot' was often the verdict.
- 49% of leaders admitted that there were policies in their organisations to discourage the cultivation of long-term relationships with partners. Yet 71% of respondents were prepared to sacrifice immediate bottom-line gain in

favour of forming long-term liaisons with organisations they trust

- There were some interesting findings on big data. Despite an unprecedented volume of data and information 65% of leaders still base decisions on human factors. 34% felt that had too much data, and 37% believed they lacked the analytical capacity to extract actionable information
- Senior women executives tend to be more rational than men, when it comes to business decisions

In the UK, Gyro conducted a different research project through YouGov. They polled 345 leaders asking them about the influence on change management of a) Empathy – feelings for other people, and b) their own Emotional responses. They divided emotional responses into positives (not many), neutral reactions (few) and negative emotional feelings (lot of them). Some highlights:

- Principal negative reactions: Worry 39%, Annoyance 30%, Disappointment 30%, Fear 24%, Anger 21%
- Principal positive reactions: Satisfaction 25%, Hope 22%, happiness 21%, Pride 19%, Joy 11%
- Southern business leaders more negative than those in the North
- Women leaders feel fewer personal positive emotional responses in themselves, and see more negative responses in others than their male equivalents

Thoughts on Spirit of Mote, the psychology of Mote, and Behavioural Economics

In recent years, most of our learning about behavioural economics and choice architecture has been about consumer choice, but the same rules should apply to our behaviour as business people, and as we juggle our lives to embrace everything we do away from work as well. We DO know how to do it. We behave to impress. We behave to please. We behave to get on and get up (think of weddings, parties, and interviews). We smile. We are sociable. We are outgoing. We try to be friendly, considerate, and civilised.

For many of us there is a shared agenda, shared belief, and shared language. We are often striving to achieve better collaboration, for example between departments, operating companies, and competing agencies. We acknowledge the need to contest the default choice of being an 'Adverso', or Devil's Advocate.

There are subtle ways in which we can incentivise good behaviour, for example by recording and videoing meetings, to encourage teams to spend less time in often futile debate and argument. We can agree to give an idea a go before trashing it, and to table points of disagreement in advance.

Process and technique give Mote a far better chance than the conventional meeting. However we also need to draw upon Behavioural Economics to 'nudge' people, particularly into behaving in a civilised and non- adverso fashion. It comes from my absolute conviction that positive behaviour and mindset is more likely to transform meetings than simply tinkering with process. It comes also from the belief that concentrating on being agreeable and conscientious is a very good goal for a typical tired and stressed business person, and also a good way of dealing with one.

It comes from seeing the meeting as a mirror of workplace behaviour in general. We are all (even the 'Neurotics') perfectly capable of behaving well when we have to (parties, interviews, important family occasions). We all (except possibly the Neurotics) get reward response from trying to behave better, argue less, and smile more, as well as approval from our superiors, peers and reports. We all know instinctively that if we behave better, others will as well, and vice versa.

Returning to the psychology of Mote, we should look to understand and embrace the concepts of Agreeableness and Conscientiousness. There is no reason to exclude characteristics of Extroversion and Openness, but we understand that the pursuit of Openness and Extraversion can (and probably will) cause controversy and make Agreeableness on all sides harder to sustain. Openness is hugely valuable in any change process, and in any project calling for innovation and creativity. But experience shows that it needs to be managed.

Similarly Extroversion is admirable and can make a big difference to selling progress and change, but a Mote process won't necessarily be aided by the 'command and control' mind-set that often goes with Extroversion. There's a 'watch out' for Leaders here, who are often extroverts to a greater or lesser degree. Too much controversy is not likely to be productive. I have always felt that two-handed lunch meetings are an excellent example of how discussion and debate can be bonding and not divisive. There's an instinct when you are with just one other person to pull back from being too critical or destructive. That's essentially what the leader has to do in a bigger Mote group.

The negativity of Neuroticism is clearly quite inappropriate for a constructive Mote. Yet how often bad meeting behaviour reflects bad temper and irritability.

It is very important to stress Agreeableness for attitude and Conscientiousness for efficiency. Society and modern business culture favour putting ideas and creativity first, being very direct, pushing back a lot, and encouraging energetic debate. Big meetings undoubtedly encourage unreasonableness and grandstanding. Politeness and restraint have become unfashionable. But how productive is it if almost every meeting becomes a pitched battle? Will human frailty be somehow 'cured' by pushy and stroppy behaviour? Does that behaviour in ourselves impress others? Or vice versa? 'Keep calm and get the details right' makes a good motto for Mote.

◆ MOTEBITE

For many of us there is a shared agenda, shared belief, and shared language.

The spirit and culture of Mote is all about teamwork and collaboration

There is an accessible lexicography to remind us and provide positive nudges:

- Keenness
- Enthusiasm
- Empathy
- Consideration
- Friendliness
- Engagement
- Commitment

Without doubt, the spirit and culture of Mote is NOT about being:

- Negative
- Adversarial
- Confrontational
- An interrupter or overtalker
- Withdrawn, quiet for long periods
- Distracted by events, people, issues outside the Mote to the point of continually texting, emailing, posting

If we take this emphasis on civilised behaviour and etiquette into the meeting room, it is in no way meant to inhibit discussion and debate. On the contrary it is intended to stimulate openness, interaction, and the best possible use of the personalities, skills and experience available. The objective is not lazy consensus, but considered alignment

◆ MOTEBITE

Being agreeable and conscientious is a very good goal for a typical tired and stressed business person, and also a good way of dealing with one.

The Spirit of Mote is at the heart of Mote. Here is a checklist:

Empathy

- Is there openness and honesty in the team?
- Is the team completely committed to the development of great solutions?
- Is there real talent (the best available talent) in the team?
- Are we proactive?
- Do we make each other stretch?
- Do we always reject the adequate in pursuit of better – and good where greatness might be achievable?

Sharing

- Do we always make time available to each other?
- Do we always share important information and developments, and make the best use of research, data and market information?
- Do we make best use of experience and related evidence?

- Do we work together to solve problems when things have gone wrong?
- Do we work collaboratively beyond the core team?

Simplicity

- Do we keep things simple, and do we manage to simplify even the complex?
- Is all our documentation clear and to the point – especially in briefing and responding to briefs?
- Once we have passed the inflection point, could each and every team member explain the solution in a ten floor elevator ride?

◆ MOTEBITE

Empathy is a very little key in one person's hands. It costs nothing, and can have a big effect on the people that person meets. But mass empathy! There is awesome power in that – enough to open several heavy doors and transform our world.

"So, everybody clear on the game plan?"

Chapter 8

THE GAME PLAN –
GETTING READY TO MOTE

Mote is a big idea and a philosophy. It is also a process. A Mote is not just a meeting. Nor is it just ONE meeting. We have to plan the SERIES of Motes, not only the first Mote. This is a task for the Navigator.

One of the most effective analogies used by Tony Crabbe in *Busy* is 'opening the file'. He writes:

'the things we normally procrastinate over are the big, difficult or creative tasks, but you can overcome this tendency by opening the file on a job a few days before you actually need to begin the work. In practice, this simply involves starting work on the problem for about 20 minutes, possibly in the form of a mind map. Then leave your subconscious to work its magic; when you finally begin the task in earnest, your thinking and ideas will really flow.'

Opening the file on a Mote is just such a flying start strategy.

What kind of a project most needs Mote?

Change management is probably the greatest challenge for leaders. It is estimated that 79% of leaders in the UK have experienced significant change in their organisations in the previous three months. It would not be an exaggeration to say that nearly all leaders are dealing with virtually continuous change.

There are three basic types of change:

- **Developmental** – doing what we do now, but doing it better. The frame of reference stays the same, but we concentrate on improvements

- **Transitional** – having a specific goal in sight, and moving from where we are to where we want to be. The destination has been decided in advance. This is a journey where we use familiar skill sets and actions such as innovation, M&A, and hiring new people

- **Transformational** – major change is needed, but this time we don't know exactly where we are going. We are going to have to get there by trial and error. A linear approach on a pre-determined schedule is unlikely to work. The change process will have to be developed in real time. Because the destination is going to be radically different from where we started out, new mind sets and behaviours will be needed to drive the necessary changes in people and culture. Envisioning the future is a challenge in itself. Finding it is a bigger challenge. Making it work is an even more serious challenge.

We will return to Transformational Change – the blue

riband event -later. Meanwhile let us look at how planning a Mote differs from planning an ordinary meeting.

How much planning and preparation went in to the last meeting you attended?

There would have been some questions asked in advance, probably along these lines: What time is the meeting? How long have we got? Can everyone stay till the end? Which room is it in? Who's going to be there? Who can't make it? Is the new guy on Wizzo able to come? Is Wayne dialling in? What time is it for him? Are we covering the problems on Fizzer and Snazzy as well as the catch-up on the rest of the portfolio?

There will have been very little about what the meeting is *for* and very little about how different our lives will be afterwards.

Mote is a theatre, so planning and preparation are critical. Would you try and put on a play without meticulous planning and rehearsal? Can you imagine coaches sending their players into big matches and tournaments without weeks of training and preparation? A live TV show? A party conference?

Yet most meetings that tie down managers and executives for hours on end do not get adequate preparation time. If you reflect on this, it is clear that if you want to be successful in external meetings (negotiations, pitches, presentations), you need to prepare with brilliant internal meetings. And if you want great internal meetings, put a priority on preparation, great care in issuing invitations, and restraint on the ground you aim to cover in the agenda. Given all of that, any meeting organiser still needs his or her fellow meeting attenders to maintain great behaviour through the day!

The Mote way – Game Plan

Dictionary definition of Game Plan – *carefully thought out strategy for achieving an objective.*

The Mote sequence will have a goal. So will each individual session. We might be looking at the sequence building up to a major decision. We might be planning a significant project. Or the task ahead might be change of one sort or another.

The Game Plan in each case will be the strategic plan for achieving the goal. Use the following checklist to organise your Game Plan:

1. Who is the Leader on this project? Who is going to be the Navigator?
2. What is our overall goal for this project? What is the nature of the decision we have to reach? What change are we setting out to achieve and manage?
3. Have we already a range of options?
4. Wording of the Motion?
5. What is the deadline for coming up with a solution? When can we start? So how much time is available to us, and how many sessions are we going to need?
6. Apart from Leader and Navigator, which Moters HAVE

to be there, and at what stage? Any remoters? Define roles and responsibilities for everyone

7. Venue and date for Pre-Mote, and session number one?

8. Pre-reads: what information, data, facts, figures, reports, evidence do we need? This should all be provided and considered at the Pre-Mote, at which Leader and Navigator will also plot the game plan for the first session, along with likely issues, opportunities and problems

9. Preferred option(s) and reward/risk analysis so far – so enabling Leader and Navigator to do a going-in assessment of the upsides and downsides of each option?

10. List of stakeholders, management and interested parties to be kept informed of progress

Setting up a Mote. Considerations for the Navigator

The Navigator is responsible for all this planning. Here is the Navigator's step-by-step guide:

STEP ONE

- Pre-Mote with Leader. Focus on why we are doing this, and what we are trying to achieve. Clarify purpose and objectives of project, and agree goal for the Mote series, and the first Mote. What decisions need to be made and when? Leader and Navigator finalise game plan

STEP TWO

- Draw up the motion (for subsequent Motes ensure

previous Mote actions are completed before finalising the motion)

STEP THREE

- Date/time/time available for the series and each Mote. Attention given to having sufficient time to do justice to the motion, while avoiding meeting congestion and back-to-backs

STEP FOUR

- Decide on venue, room. Ideally no compact Motes should be held in huge rooms

STEP FIVE

- Look at required resource – skills, knowledge, and experience. Decide on which Moters to invite to deliver this, and whether to add remoters. For second and subsequent Motes, Navigator will be using stepladder to add Moters selectively, and stand them down when their contributions have been made

STEP SIX

- Send out meeting invitations – and briefing on process and behaviour. Decide on what pre-reads are required

STEP SEVEN

- Set up meeting space, and ensure all necessary equipment is available (including telecomms for patching in remoters)

STEP EIGHT
- Navigator prepares own contribution and makes sure Leader's is ready to go, including the dynamic opener

STEP NINE
- Navigator rehearses content and running order, and calculates timing. Issue pre-reads to Moters, and communicate with other stakeholders as necessary

STEP TEN
- Prepare template for filing Mote reporting

How does this set-up procedure differ from what would normally be done ahead of a conventional meeting? Call it a Mote, and it is already a different experience – with enhanced expectations for everyone involved. Mote is a much more controlled and deliberate process, and has to be organised quite differently from a conventional meeting. With meetings the focus is on logistics, making sure as many people as possible turn up, and supplying the coffee. Motes are about performance and results – so preparation is everything.

i.   That's why there is a Leader to drive the series and each session, and a Navigator to keep things on track
ii. And why Mote is a much smaller meeting than we are used to
iii. Leader and Navigator must be committed to planning the session and achieving the desired outcome
iv. Choice of Moters/remoters is absolutely critical. Not

only is it essential to have the right people on board, it is vital to have them in the Mote and in good shape, which means a brilliantly run session, and no back-to-backs!

v. So liaison with actual and potential Moters is also part of the Navigator's responsibility, telling them what is expected of all participants in a Mote

vi. This includes briefing them on the principles and spirit of Mote:

   a. Planning and preparation

   b. Scheduling and timing to execute the motion

   c. Targeted outputs and outcomes

   d. Collaborative approach – teamwork, not individual initiative

   e. Empathic behaviour – nothing disruptive or adversarial

   f. High level meeting etiquette

   g. Overall – commitment, discipline and positivity

vii. It is up to the Leader to deflect FOMO (fear of missing out) by reassuring stakeholders NOT invited to each Mote that the process is strong – and they will be kept informed

◆ MOTEBITE

Call it a Mote, and it is already a different experience – with enhanced expectations for everyone involved

Meticulous preparation sorts out a Mote from the average meeting

Confucius wrote (around 500 BC), 'Success depends upon previous preparation, and without such preparation there is sure to be failure'. I wonder how many meetings he had to endure during his extraordinary life and travels. It is well worth recording his ethical spin on the Golden Rule (sometimes dubbed the Silver Rule): 'What you do not wish for yourself, do not do to others.'

Most books about meeting practice, best practice courses, and the majority of meeting experts, concentrate on the minutiae of actually running a meeting. There are very few that give good counsel on what happens after a meeting is over. Almost none advocate meticulous preparation, rehearsal and orchestration.

◆ MOTEBITE

'Success depends upon previous preparation, and without such preparation there is sure to be failure' – Confucius

Planning when the Mote is about decision-making

This Mote will be about a substantial project. The clear goal is a big decision. Effectively that will be the only item on the Motion (agenda). The Mote needs to start before the beginning of the Mote! Pre-planning is vital. For the Mote to have a positive outcome and valuable outputs, it needs a stream of appropriate inputs (data, information, analysis etc). We can usually only achieve that by holding a Pre-Mote, or a number of Pre-Motes. We need to map out the Mote in advance. And that starts by asking a series of questions.

What is the goal we are trying to achieve by making the decision?

How long have we got to make the decision? There might be an aspect which we can get to in 60 minutes, which just happens to be the average time of most meetings. But it is more likely to be a 60 hour decision (Mon-Thurs)? Or even a 60 day decision (brief in March, report back in May. It can't be a 60 second decision, because we'd already be too late! Obviously the Mote must be allocated enough time, and if necessary as many sessions as are needed.

Are there problems that have to be solved before we can make a decision? We have to remember that decisions by themselves don't solve problems.

Even more crucially are there any opportunities we can identify? Agree what the opportunities are, and we are half way to working out the options. Are we sure what the opportunity is? Or are we sure what the problem is? If it's an opportunity, have we identified it correctly, and do we know how we are going to take advantage of it? If it's a problem, do we know precisely what it is, and how to solve it?

So what is our goal? This must be exactly what we are looking for our decision to achieve. Unless everyone concerned with a decision knows what the goal is, you cannot assess the wisdom of a decision or particular course of action. Is pursuing this goal a team task? In which case have we got the right team on the case?

Having agreed on the opportunity or problem, and set a goal, it is then time to look at options: how many possible answers are there? What are these options? Are we sure we have explored all the meaningful ones? Is there enough data and information to analyse each of the options, and can we get more if needs be? We need to leave reasonable time here (if available) for gathering and analysing information and intelligence. Control what we can, and we must do our best to predict what we can't.

Have we looked at the upsides and downsides of each option? For each option we need to write down the best upside (highest reward) and the worst potential downside (biggest risk). If it isn't immediately obvious what is the most compelling route, first look at the worst downside, and eliminate that route, unless the upside is particularly alluring. Then look at the upsides in order of attractiveness. We are looking for the best balance.

What looks to be the best decision?

These are the ten steps up to, but not including taking the decision itself:

Steps 1–3: To be discussed in the Pre-Mote

Step 4: Having been rigorous in interrogating the opportunity or problem, we should be in shape to define the goal, in pursuit of which we have to make a decision. Committing to a goal is absolutely essential. Neither capitalising on an opportunity nor solving a problem is of itself going to be the goal. We have to know what we're aiming at. It's essential to communicate this at the outset of the Mote.

Steps 5-10: The essence of the rational side of the Smart Decision process. Every step is important for all decisions except the ones that have to be made instantly, or very quickly.

Steps 1-10: This is as far as you can take a purely rational approach. We still need to:

- Think about how to communicate the decision
- And crucially how to implement it – initially and ongoing, which will inevitably involve feedback, more intelligence, and more decisions

But vitally we must also account for gut feel before making the decision. How do we do this? Obviously initial reactions to the options wouldn't all be driven by logic. One of the options will almost certainly have been more attractive, as even when we are at our most rigorous, it is difficult to be completely cold and analytical. Just as steps 1-10 will have given us a winner *in the mind*, we will almost certainly also have a winner *in the heart*. Hopefully – but by no means always – the same one.

So we start by agreeing two targets – our overall goal, and exactly what kind of decision we need from the forthcoming Mote. The Pre-Mote is where we not only look at data, but also at problems, opportunities, and a first list of options. It helps the progress of the Mote itself to get as much problem-solving as possible out of the way offline from the Mote. Meetings – particularly big meetings – are notoriously inefficient at solving problems. Too many people, too many views, often too little focus, and a dose of individuals wanting to shine make for an unpromising cocktail. Solving key problems, or at least moving them on the road to solution, at Pre-Mote stage is both immensely useful and a tremendous time-saver down the line.

But it is in the area of identifying opportunities that the Pre-More really comes into its own. The options we look at in a Mote en route to a decision are very much a function of the opportunities that we have identified. Many decisions are effectively realised opportunities.

How do we decide who attends the Mote? To start with every Mote needs a Leader. Not a chair. This is an action-orientated gathering, not a talking shop. It must be the Leader's responsibility to kick it off and manage it throughout. It is the Leader's ultimate goal to ensure the Mote produces a decision.

To make this happen the Leader needs his/her partner – the Navigator. The Navigator's role is to steer the group towards its objective, and also to ensure it doesn't get distracted and go off course. The Navigator has another vital task, to referee proceedings, and keep the group within the rules. In a Mote it also makes sense for the Navigator to be the scribe, and to summarise progress and what has been achieved.

◆ MOTEBITE
The Mote needs to start before the beginning of the Mote!

Profiling the team

As soon as we accept that a Mote consists of a team, not just a connection of individuals, attendees or participants, other factors come into play. The most important of these is profiling. In the context of Mote this needs to happen in advance of specific sessions. Understanding personality profiles of actual and potential team members is an important ingredient of casting.

For many years I have used a version of a popular personality profiling model as a key diagnostic to help our clients find agencies that suited them. We have also used it extensively in our relationship management practice to provide people-based solutions in cases of malfunctioning client/agency situations. Surprisingly few agencies use profiling in either selling or servicing to help create better chemistry with clients.

As with most models, we use four primary groupings, which can be combined in any combination of two for people who are not clearly one type.

The model (which I call the Headline system) is based on the classic DISC model, invented by William Moulton Marston. The typologies in common use in the 1980s business world were Drivers, Expressives, Amiables and

Analysts. This model was adapted for advertising agencies by Stuart Sanders, a consultant from Richmond Virginia, to help his agency clients better understand themselves and what made their clients and prospects tick. I first met Sanders in London in 1990, and worked with him on a number of projects thereafter, mainly in the US. The version of Sanders's model illustrated below owes much to the development work of Mike Longhurst, Senior VP in McCann-Erickson EMEA, based in London. Sanders's clever contribution was to use advertising terms to bring the typologies to life, and also to devise a methodology by which trained agency new business specialists could profile their opposite numbers using all sorts of observation tests, without asking them to fill in a questionnaire (impractical), and without the clients realising what was going on. McCann developed and updated this for international use. Sanders's material was mainly US-focused. They also devised a straightforward non-technical self-profiling questionnaire. The four types (with descriptions tailored to client marketing executives) in the Headline model are as follows (with explanatory diagrams below):

Headline – typical CEO type. A driver who makes things happen. Good delegator, but makes the decisions him / herself. Demanding, often intolerant and totally task-oriented. Makes well-informed, but ultimately intuitive decisions. Likes authority, leadership, drive, energy, compliance with their wishes.

Illustration – can be a global brand director type. Outgoing, mercurial, inspirational, entertaining and with good people skills. Likes to be part of the agency team and feels very creative. Must see big ideas, excitement, optimism, fun.

Logo – typical "nice person". Gains power and influence by getting on with people. Likeable, honest, fair and a great team worker / leader. Likes consensus, relaxed style, no controversy / risk. Wants to get to know people he/she work with personally.

Body Copy – typical Marketing Manager / Director type. A professional. High on knowledge but can be low on taking responsibility. Often with poor people skills, but gets by through being the one with the knowledge. Likes detail, info, strategy, keeping on top of complexity.

Orientation

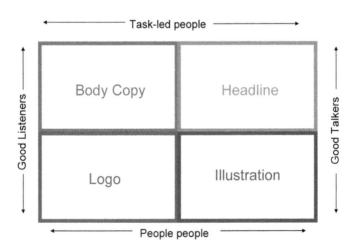

Personality

Analytical Detailed Precise Thorough Cautious	Short attention Straight to business Demanding Decisive Fairly formal
Very welcoming Likes to get to know Hospitable Appreciative Team-builder	Great fun Easy to get to know Very sociable Enthusiastic Inspirational

How they get things done

Assemble the facts Analyse Write a recommendation Rational process Research	Take the lead Give clear instructions Delegate Set targets / dates / incentives / rewards
Form a team Hold frequent meetings Discuss openly Build consensus Share responsibility	Define the vision Blue sky solutions Sometimes impractical Change mind Have fun

What they like

Process / Methodologies Experience Case histories Strategic development Research / test results	Their person (who they call) Senior management Be brief / decisive Results Costs and timings
Meet "Their team" Get to know you Teamwork Human interest Meetings	The creatives Big names Awards Entertainment The big vision / idea

The guiding principle of the way we have used this profiling system is that people want to work with people like them. This is particularly true of Headlines and Illustrations. The strength of Logos is they can get on with anyone. Body Copies accept that many of the colleagues, bosses and people in other companies will be from other typologies, because that is the way of big organisations (but they do enjoy working with other Body Copies). The real HR world is obviously more complex than four typologies can do justice. There are more possible typologies than the basic four:

- Intensified characteristics: Headline / Headlines, Illustration / Illustrations and so forth
- Headline / Body Copies, Body Copy / Headlines,

Headline / Illustrations, Illustration / Logos, Logo / Illustrations, Logo / Body Copies and Body Copy / Logos. Personalities only very rarely stretch across the diagonals.

There are of course numerous other personality profiling methods in use, notably Myers Briggs and 16pf. My purpose in featuring the Headline system is based on close personal experience and the fact that it was fashioned around the ad industry.

◆ MOTEBITE

Profiling is indispensable for maximising people's potential in a team environment like Mote

Ambitious goals demand careful preparation, careful preparation needs Mote, the Mote needs great casting – but you still need empathy and the Spirit of Mote.

American business guru Marshall Goldsmith published *What got you here won't get you there* in 2007. He tells compelling stories about clever people who have either lost their personal GPS mechanism, or are facing such formidable change management tasks that they need coaching and reorientation. In every case just doing is not enough. Leaders need to do three things, according to Goldsmith – prepare brilliantly, take their people with them, and look to their own behaviour.

The preparation required is the game planning described

above. Mote provides the 'thinking together' environment to utilise the ability of stakeholders and colleagues. Being honest about flaws in interpersonal behaviour, and being prepared to do something about it, is crucial to success or failure. Goldsmith instanced '20 bad habits'. He didn't call them '20 bad habits in meetings', but he might just as well have, because it is in the meeting environment that most of this behaviour comes through. Here are the 20:

1. The need to win at all costs
2. Insisting on trying to add value to every discussion
3. Rating others and imposing our standards on them
4. Making destructive comments
5. Starting every intervention with 'No', 'But', or 'However'
6. Telling the world how smart we are
7. Speaking when angry
8. 'Let me explain why this won't work'
9. Refusing to share important information
10. Failing to give proper praise and reward
11. Claiming credit that we don't deserve
12. Making excuses
13. Clinging to the past
14. Failing to see when we are treating someone unfairly
15. Refusing to express regret
16. Not listening
17. Failing to express gratitude
18. Punishing the messenger

19. Passing the buck
20. Excessive need to be 'me'

Sometimes we can listen to an expert and feel an onrush of support for their views. On other occasions we read a litany of criticism of behaviours and attitudes, and have that sinking feeling that it is me they are talking about. I must admit to frequent failings over the years on at least 17 of the above! Krznaric wrote *Empathy* several years after Goldsmith's *What Got You Here Won't Get You There*, but there's a real compatibility between the conviction of both the American leadership coach and the British cultural thinker that to succeed you have to be prepared to put yourself in the other person's shoes.

◆ MOTEBITE

Even with good planning, feet of clay can sabotage process. But Mote provides an environment where leaders can behave empathetically and motivate their people to rise to a big challenge.

Chapter 9

HOW TO MANAGE A MOTE, AND RUN THE BEST MEETING EVER

Preparation of the Mote is indeed crucial, and follow-up is vital, but you only get one chance to run a Mote brilliantly, and that is in real time. This chapter is about the synergistic roles of Leader, Navigator, Moters and remoters in driving progress. It all starts with two people – Leader and Navigator

Two can do (almost) anything

If he can say as you can
Guinness is good for you
How grand to be a Toucan
Just think what Toucan do

This legendary campaign by SH Benson for Guinness first saw the light of day in the late 1920's, with none other than Dorothy L Sayers as the copywriter. 'Just think what Toucan do' was a great slogan for Guinness, but today it would have suffered the same fate (for encouraging too much consumption) as the even more famous 'Guinness is good for you', which it probably isn't. I like the slogan because I worked out a long time ago that a dynamic duo is by far the most efficient grouping. Better balanced than even the most outstanding individual (few old sayings are as true as 'two heads are better than one'). More agile and higher performing than conference rooms full of clever people. Faux democracy has much to answer for when meetings of all the 'right people' fail to deliver.

The moment you see lots of chairs around a table in a meeting room, take time to reflect that the meeting problem has already started. Think of all those egos, all those agendas, the attraction of speaking over listening, the influence of the loudest, the marginalisation of the quieter ones. Whereas a determined twosome can make dramatic progress in moving a project forward, or towards a decision. Capitalise on the Power of One (Leader) to produce strong ideas and the ability of a Dynamic Duo (Leader and Navigator) to take an idea forward at pace.

The Navigator's job is to keep the Mote on plan, and tightly in line with the Motion. Also to support the Leader – and encourage all the Moters to use their skills, knowledge and energy to contribute to outstanding team performance and behaviour.

◆ MOTEBITE

A dynamic duo is by far mankind's most efficient grouping.

Casting / Stepladder

Leader and Navigator are the lynchpins of Mote. Other participants – the Moters and remoters – need to be brought on board by the Stepladder system. So now that we have conducted the Pre-Mote, and the Leader and Navigator are in position, what happens next? I have already written about Stepladder. It was originally a problem-solving technique that worked by adding one person at a time, and only when you need an extra player. Of course we can always add further experts at any time in the process. But the additional team members can, and should, leave the stage after they have been able to add value. Casting needs to be on the basis of function, rank, expertise, responsibility and so on – but also by considering complementary profiles and roles using the Belbin Team Roles Model, as explained in chapter 6.

Balancing the team and identifying roles

The 'Headline' system is invaluable for helping us to understand what makes each member of the team tick, and from Sanders's work and our own experience we know how powerful it is to put like with like. A Mote is basically a small team, and it's key to ensure it has Moters and remoters with complementary attributes and skills. The Belbin system can be used before a project starts to maximise balance. As the Mote series develops, Leader and Navigator can observe the individual members of the team, and see how they behave, contribute and behave within the team. The Belbin approach can also help shed light on how one or more team members could improve how they work together and with others to avoid potential conflict of their natural styles. It is also useful to establish whether new skills need to be brought onto the team to cover weaknesses.

Once the team is chosen and organised, the group can move into action

There are three stages of collaborative activity in a Mote. *Thinking together* is the innovatory launch pad. We can use the intellectual power, experience, expertise of the Moters to come collectively to solutions, instead of wasting time and dissipating energy in debate. The Mote (let's say it is the third in this particular series) is due to start at 10.30am. 90 minutes have been allocated. Leader, Navigator and three Moters are around the table. One of the Moters is new to the group having been introduced on the Stepladder system. There is some small talk and banter as everyone waits for the Remoter in Dubai to dial in. We have already had a pre-Mote and two full sessions. Why do we need to start by Thinking Together? Can't we simply dive in and work together?

There are two main reasons: first, less time will be wasted if great thinking precedes 'getting the job done'. Secondly, collaboration and the Spirit of Mote will be enhanced during the next two stages by having thought together and achieved consensus and joint ownership of the thinking.

Working together is achieving the change, coming to the decision, and driving the project forward.

Succeeding and Winning together consists of taking progress in the room towards implementation and success in the world outside.

Taking a decision or solution out of the room it was made in is a crucial step, because you have to tell people what has been decided by communicating it internally, and externally, as necessary. Then there's the question of implementing it, what experts call making the decision right, or proving the solution. Every decision is a journey, and we may need a Plan B, and sometimes a Plan C and D as well, to cope with changing circumstances, mistakes, disasters, competitive action, and so forth. And talking of mistakes and disasters, we have to allow for learning and feedback. We learn to walk by falling over. We learn as much from the decisions that don't work out as from those that do.

◆ MOTEBITE

No one became a great decision maker by getting it right every time.

The hard yards in Mote pay off, given collaborative behaviour

Conventional meetings are normally free-flow. Motes have to be planned in advance as we have seen above, and carefully orchestrated once under way. The Leader has to take the initiative and start things off with a dynamic opener, and also rise to the challenge at the end with a dynamic close. The Navigator has to work hard throughout keeping the Mote on track.

For Developmental Change Moters can move straight into Working together. The objective is to change from an unsatisfactory or merely adequate way of doing something in the organisation to an improved process or system. Both the goal and the nature of the journey have been established. There are some 'who?', 'when?', 'what?', 'where?' questions to be posed and answered, but delivering the project efficiently within the Mote process should be reasonably straightforward. The group will be outputting from the outset.

For Transitional Change a destination will have already been identified at the planning stage, but the journey is less obvious, and Moters need to start by Thinking together, gathering new inputs, analysing and strategising. This is more complicated than Developmental change. But given good Leadership and Navigation and judicious use of Stepladder to make sure the right people are in the room, it should not be long before the inflection point, and the transition to Working Together.

Transformational Change represents a different scale of challenge. Neither destination nor journey is clear. The title of Goldsmith's book *What got you here won't get you there* sums up the situation perfectly. Almost everything may need to change – culture, people, systems, process, scale. Even fundamental markers like purpose and mission may need to be recast. There are quite likely to be big financial issues, also HR implications, and negotiations with government, regulators and unions. This is the kind of task and challenge for which Mote was invented. Goldsmith didn't know about Mote, but he is very mindful of the need for leaders to involve stakeholders, managers, suppliers, customers etc, and to be empathic and collaborative, rather than dictatorial.

He conducted a massive survey of 11,000 leaders in eight multinationals on four continents and discovered that taking people with you is far more likely to be successful than refusing to dialogue, but largely for Spirit of Mote reasons. 95% of the leaders who dialogued with stakeholders measurably improved their interpersonal behaviour and chances of success. The leaders who walked alone unsurprisingly carried on behaving badly, and their chances of achieving successful outcomes were barely above random.

Good conversation skills are vital

Meeting gurus and coaches emphasise the importance of good conversation in meetings. Alan Barker, author of

How to Manage Meetings, describes meeting conversation as 'a dynamic of talking and listening. These two activities do not happen merely in sequence, but simultaneously: each participant in a conversation both speaks and listens throughout the conversation. Our effectiveness in a conversation depends both on how well we talk and on how well we listen'. In a memorable phrase he describes conversation as 'turn-taking'.

Barker lists seven strategies for improving the quality of conversation in meetings:

- Improve your listening skills
  - He suggests conducting an 'internal conversation' in your own head while you are listening and others are talking

- Structure your thinking
  - He recommends 'first stage' thinking about the problem...
  - ...and 'second stage' thinking about the solution

- Manage time
  - A major responsibility for a chair in a conventional meeting and for the Navigator in a Mote

- Find common ground
  - An essential lubricant to getting on well and making progress. Think of a lunch situation or a party encounter

- – Who do you know in common? What part of the
  world are you both familiar with?
- – This gives permission to share a subject, or possibly a
  warning light to dangerous territory

- Move beyond argument
  - – Some would say that argument (or 'debate') is the
    default setting for meeting conversation. But it is not
    an ideal basis for making progress
  - – Barker quotes Chris Argyris, (1923-2013, a pathfinding
    Harvard organisational psychologist) who invented
    the Ladder of Inference. The Ladder allows you to
    step down from assumptions and opinions, and to
    avoid conflict by climbing back up towards shared
    beliefs by using past experience to make sense
    of issues which might otherwise be relentlessly
    confrontational
  - – Argyris didn't habitually refer to empathy, but his
    teaching was very much within the Spirit of Mote

- Summarise often
  - – Summarising is a vital part of the meeting
    conversationalist's armoury
  - – Summarising manages time
  - – Summarising helps establish common ground
  - – Summarising allows us to refer back to problems and
    goals, while looking ahead to solutions and winning
    through

- Use visuals
  - Barker says that apparently we remember only 20% of what we hear, but 80% of what we see. So the judicious use of visual aids can materially help communication
  - Dr Haig Kouyoumdjian posted this piece on the Get Psyched! Blogsite in July 2012 – 'A large body of research indicates that visual cues help us to better retrieve and remember information. The research outcomes on visual learning make complete sense when you consider that our brain is mainly an image processor (much of our sensory cortex is devoted to vision), not a word processor. In fact, the part of the brain used to process words is quite small in comparison to the part that processes visual images'.

Asking questions can make a Mote even more effective

Many books about meetings focus on conversation technique, but numbers of people talking is not always the most effective way of making progress. Asking questions can be a better way. Tony Crabbe introduced me to the ultimate Question guru – Mike Marquardt.

Dr Michael Marquardt is Professor of Human Resource Development and International Affairs at George Washington University in DC, where he is additionally Program Director of Overseas Programs. He is also President of the World Institute for Action Learning. Marquardt has published many books and even more widely referenced papers. But his 2005 book *Leading With Questions* is the most significant in the context of meetings. The subtitle is *How Leaders Find the Right Solutions by Knowing What to Ask.*

Marquardt believes that leadership is not about knowing all the answers, and talking a lot. It's about knowing what great questions to ask, and carefully listening to those answers. This book is a piece of management wisdom that shows leaders how to ask great questions – questions that inspire, motivate and empower the organisation. It's about developing a culture where asking questions is safe and desired. This corresponds with the core philosophy of Action Learning – 'People being aware of their lack of relevant knowledge, and being prepared to explore the area of their ignorance with suitable questions and help from other people in similar positions'.

If we go back to the 'Cleverness Illusion' and 'Stakeholder Saturation' that we identified earlier, we concluded that it is a fallacy that a group of clever involved people will necessarily put their heads together and come up with good ideas.

Marquardt suggests that meeting participants should – as an alternative to selling an idea – challenge colleagues to say why the idea *won't* work. Then listen carefully to what people say. This legitimises the selling of doubts and shifts the process from selling to co-creation. He says, 'give everyone a chance to speak by going around the room and asking where people stand on an issue'. He points out correctly that it is common for conversations to be dominated by one or two people. Hearing from everyone often shifts the conversation and allows you to bring closure to an issue.

Another suggestion, 'Ask questions at the end of every meeting':

- How well has this session gone?
- What has the group done well?
- What could the group do better?
- What are we not doing that we could be doing?
- What actions are we going to take as a group next time that will improve our performance?

Marquardt identifies different kinds of question:

- Open-ended – what possibilities come to mind?
- Clarification – are you saying...or...?
- Questions for details – what have you tried so far?
- Stimulating questions – have you asked x what his concerns are?
- Probing questions – why did this happen?
- Summarising questions – what is the major point that has been made here?

He goes on to say, 'Of course, many leaders do ask questions constantly—questions such as these: Why are you behind schedule? Who isn't keeping up? What's the problem with this project? Whose idea was that? Too often, we ask questions that disempower rather than empower our subordinates. These questions cast blame; they are not genuine requests for information. Other sorts of questions are often no more than thinly veiled attempts at manipulation: Don't you agree with me on that? Aren't you a team player? If you tend to ask these sorts of questions, this book is for you. So the point isn't that leaders just don't ask enough questions. Often, we don't ask the right questions. Or we don't ask questions in a way that will lead to honest and informative answers. Many of us don't know how to listen effectively to the answers to questions—and haven't established a climate in which asking questions is encouraged. And that's where this book comes in. The purpose of Leading with Questions is to help you become a stronger leader by learning how to ask the right questions effectively, how to listen effectively, and how to create a climate in which asking questions becomes as natural as breathing.'

The Leader's job is to drive and not chair. The Navigator is a performance director in a meeting environment. The Moters are present as team players dedicated to ensuring each Mote is a success, as well as the project as a whole. Motes are about outputs and outcomes – not just inputs and free flow discussion. Motes are about solutions and progress – not questions and problems.

Both Motes and meetings are about discussion and debate, but Motes are dedicated to what the debate produces, not just to providing a forum for people's views. Motes are about reaching considered alignment, not lazy consensus So the management of a Mote is dedicated to achievement, success and enhancing the decision making process.

Motes do not always run smoothly, despite Spirit of Mote

If a Moter (or worse the Leader or Navigator) fails to make the Mote or has to leave early it can be disastrous. It also frequently happens that dominant personalities talk all the time – if this happens it is a challenge for the Navigator.

Sometimes in meetings as many as 50% of attendees make very little contribution, and that would be a real problem for a Mote, considering that every player has been hand-picked.

Players may not have been listening closely enough. The Mote might have moved forward before one or more problems have been solved. Opportunities have been missed – or worse, not recognised. Players have not had access to all the available data or information, or it has not been presented clearly or in an unbiased way. Disagreements may have become apparent and not resolved, which may make unanimity difficult to achieve. Time has run out before the Mote comes to a Decision.

There's no magic formula. We need to practise and do exercises to learn how to overcome these problems. Rest assured there are solutions to all the above issues.

Finally there's poor Mote etiquette – overtalking, going off piste, forgetting the importance of reaching a Decision, and falling into traditional meeting behaviour. Even in a Mote there can be troublemakers not acting in keeping with the Spirit, and you have to identify these people and deal with the problem.

Great meeting technique doesn't need high technology

Neil Sandy who is COO of Truestone Impact Investment Management is a friend and business associate of mine. I have been working with Neil on a start-up. He is an unquestioned master of the whiteboard.

Every book on meetings counsels producing a checklist to make sure we have remembered all the key points. Neil goes one better. He uses the whiteboard to map the meeting like some kind of corporate satnav. He starts his meetings with an interactive discussion on goals, timing and process, recording everything we agree on the whiteboard, and producing visual minutes in real time throughout. At the end of the meeting he takes everyone through the complete 'map', establishes consensus, allocates follow-up activity, and then photographs the whiteboard on his phone. As the meeting breaks up, he wipes the board clean, and by the time we have all returned to our desks, the picture of the whiteboard is in our inbox.

Twenty tips for running more successful Motes

1. Accept Daniel Levitin's view that multi-tasking doesn't work. Start the meeting with a ban on devices, form a phone stack, stick with one motion, and sustain maximum concentration all round.

2. Or if you are nervous about coming across as too

schoolmasterly, start instead with some round the room play, and then make the phone stack another game.

3. Be single-minded by all means, but always develop other options, and solutions that may be less risky or controversial. There is no cop out in insisting that a Mote has a Plan B up its sleeve.

4. This is also true of Motes that are essentially negotiations. Negotiation is about finding a workable agreement that can satisfy both parties. Find a compromise that everyone can accept and offer more than one option.

5. Remember the essential De Bono principle of lateral thinking – the less obvious idea may have more potential. It is far more collaborative to kick around more ideas, than to spend endless time and energy debating between A and B, and then booting B into the long grass.

6. Improve critical thinking in the group by encouraging everyone to think of the opposite from time to time.

7. Use the Tony Crabbe mantra of taking frequent breaks to keep people fresh, galvanise the performance of the group, and give people no excuse to lose concentration. Help everyone get in the zone and stay there.

8. Also try Crabbe's killer question 'What problem are we are trying to solve?' the moment the group starts going

off-piste. 'What is the breakthrough opportunity?' is another good question.

9. 'Throw away what isn't excellent'. This is the mantra of Simon Clift, Unilever's first global CMO (Chief Marketing Officer), when describing the creative process in advertising. It applies equally to all meetings, and to Motes in particular.

10. Encourage note-taking, because of all the psychological evidence that it helps retention. Use the Chinese proverb, 'The faintest ink beats the strongest memory'.

11. Eating together not only keeps people going. It also puts people on the same level. You can use refreshments to improve bonding.

12. Don't overload Moters with too much data. Remember Gerd Gigerenzer's 'beneficial degree of ignorance' – the instinctive response to tricky questions and dilemmas.

13. Make your Mote more effective by persuading your Moters to clear time before and after the session, so they are not distracted by what happened at the meeting before, or by opening the file on the one to follow. Remember that back to back meetings help no one – the organisation, the participants, meeting organisers. To Mote effectively, Moters need to secure their own time before and after Motes.

14. If there is any choice, when planning a Mote sequence, for something really difficult like Transformational

Change that needs deep concentration, go for fewer, longer Motes. With normal projects and Developmental Change, shorter Motes will work better.

15. In longer meetings regular short directive breaks ('5 minutes to check your emails') can be very effective. Evidence is that people start brighter after a break. Interestingly the Start-Stop system in modern cars appears to boost concentration as well as reducing pollution, and, possibly, saving fuel (opinions differ!).

16. Inspiring venues can work better if the stakes are higher, particularly if the venue reflects the core aspects of the decision being made.

17. If the Mote is about changing behaviour at work, remember how resistant people can be. Don't expect instant responses. Ask for a small change first.

18. People can resent being excluded from meetings they are accustomed to attending. Make sure communications to stakeholders are regular, effective and motivating.

19. 'Too long, didn't read' (tl; dr) is undoubtedly a factor in this fast-paced, confusing world. Attention spans are shorter. Longer presentations, briefings and documentation are probably less effective than ten years ago.

20. Motes are about reaching considered alignment, not lazy consensus. However collaborative the attitude, however empathic the behaviour in a Mote, we still

need solutions, and results that work. Don't try and coach Moters into conformity. Empathy is one thing, being a pussycat is another. Mote works because of discussion, conversation and rigour.

◆ MOTEBITE

Running a Mote is as skilful as coaching a football team or directing a play

"But no progress in meeting."

Chapter 10

IDEAS INTO ACTION – THE MOTE ISN'T OVER WHEN IT'S OVER

Now to make sure the Mote starts to work *outside* the meeting room. After all the great thinking and concerted effort, it is vital it delivers in spades.

Once most meetings are over, the conference room empties (a process that may have started even earlier), the dramatis personae disperse and the leave behind is often no more substantial than the unwiped whiteboard and the coffee cups that didn't quite make it into the bin. In many ways that is exactly what is wrong with meetings as we know them. The effort in setting up a meeting, and the time committed to it by a lot of people is very often disproportionately greater than the return.

How does Mote deliver results in the change management scenario?

If we revisit Developmental Change, Transitional Change and Transformational Change, the 'after game' differs markedly in each case.

a) Developmental

A Mote or a series of Motes designed to manage an improvement project should be extremely effective. A pre-determined journey and outcome should make for a very positive outcome. Stakeholders will have been involved from the beginning, but on an 'as and when' basis through Stepladder, so as not to promote too conservative an approach. Developmental change is less dramatic, but it is still change – and change for a good reason. Even before the end of the Mote sequence aspects of the change programme will probably have already been put into practice. In any case the gap between decision/solution and implementation will be a very short one. Mote will have delivered change rapidly.

b) Transitional

The outcome will have been predicated, but not the journey, so timelines will have been less controllable, and some degree of falling behind schedule is quite likely. Nonetheless the destination has been known from the beginning, and so implementation will have been planned to some level.

c) Transformational

Quite possibly in the case of a truly transformational project, the outcome will have been very difficult to predict with any degree of accuracy. The team knew from the outset that something quite new was needed, but not quite what, not quite how, nor quite when. Both journey, means and ultimate destination were up for discussion in a testing series of Motes. Getting to an inspiring solution will have been one big challenge. Codifying it won't have been easy, and implementation is probably going to be complicated, given the sheer magnitude of change.

You can't afford to wait until the Mote is over!

Implementation needs to be planned ahead of time to effectively take the win out of the Mote and into the real world. By definition change management involves moving from where we are to where we want to be, and once we have the destination in sight we need to be clear about what we do when we get there. Nor is it simply a question of what we *do*. Who do we need to communicate with? What do we need to tell them? When? How? What will we need to do next?

Having seen each Mote sequence as a three stage process (before, during, and after), we now realise the 'after' has three phases as well – first, anticipating reaching our destination; secondly formally celebrating bringing the Mote to a successful conclusion; and thirdly, follow-up activity. Let's look at this through the eyes of the Navigator.

After every individual Mote the Navigator has some questions to answer

PROGRESS
- Was the outcome what we needed?
- Did we achieve our goal in the Mote?

- Are we on track to hit the objectives for the series of Motes as a whole?
- Have we a decision in view, or are we nearer to it?
- Have I summarised progress on paper in a way that does justice to the contribution of everyone present, and the curiosity and legitimate interests of stakeholders who were not there?

PROCESS

- Did we stick to our plan, and make the best use of time?
- Did stepladder work well?
- Did we do a good job in sharing important information and developments, and make the best use of research, data and market information?
- Did we make best use of experience and related evidence?
- Did we work together to solve problems as they arose?
- Did everyone have access to all available data or information?
- Has it been presented clearly, and in an unbiased way
- Were there any disagreements that have now become apparent? Are these still unresolved? And is there a danger that this may make unanimity difficult to achieve?
- Are we on track with the decision timetable?

PERFORMANCE

- Did we do everything to ensure a successful performance, in terms of thinking together and working together?

- Was every aspect different from a normal meeting – and that bit better?
- Did I support the Leader, and help him/her to inspire and direct?
- Was the teamwork good?
- Did individual Moters do well?

SPIRIT OF MOTE

- Was the atmosphere positive, constructive and friendly?
- Did we make time to allow everyone to contribute?
- Did we work collaboratively, and avoid the obvious meeting errors – adversarial behaviour, overtalking, interrupting etc?

NEXT MOTE

- What can we learn from this Mote that will help us make the next session even more fruitful? Will it give a flying start to the next Mote?
- Outline motion for the next Mote
- Indications on which Moters/remoters should be brought in/released on the Stepladder principle
- Things to try in the next round

SPREADING THE WORD

- Have we communicated the outcome to the stakeholders and everyone who needs to know?
- What about those with a fear of missing out? Are we continuing to keep them motivated, and suitably grateful for having time back in their lives?

Once the Mote sequence has been completed, the Navigator has the same routine to fulfil in respect of the final Mote session, as well as for the Mote sequence as a whole. The big difference at the end of the Mote sequence is looking forward to implementation, as opposed to the next Mote. As noted above, the Navigator will already have anticipated a successful conclusion to the series of Motes. Having thought together and worked together, the Mote team have succeeded and won together.

Does the post mortem on a Mote differ from that on a conventional meeting?

Completely! After the average meeting you normally have some minutes (mainly consisting of what various people said), and the date of the next meeting.

After a Mote you have:

- A write-up of what the meeting has achieved
- An analysis of how efficient it was
- An analysis of how the Moters performed
- A rating of collaboration, empathy, good behaviour and etiquette
- Communications, as necessary
- A blueprint for the next Mote

Every decision is a journey. Once the decision has been made, it needs to be communicated. Implementers will be enlisted. The decision will have to be tracked, to assure performance, and there will be learning and feedback. The proof of a Mote lies in the way the decision is communicated, executed, managed through, and how and what we learn from it. There's no magic formula. Just as the challenge is different for every Mote, so is implementation and learning.

◆ MOTEBITE

After the average meeting you normally have some minutes (mainly consisting of what various people said), and the date of the next meeting. After each Mote you are one step nearer to your goal. Once the Mote sequence is completed, you have won!

"Okay, let's get this mote on the road."

LAUNCHING MOTE INTO THE ORGANISATION

Mote isn't a theoretical app for making dynamic and strategic meetings more productive. It's a completely practical system that you can start experimenting with very quickly, provided you are ready to offer essential training for Leaders, Navigators and Moters. Here is how you can start to transform the efficiency of meetings in your company.

We need permission to start changing the meeting habits of a lifetime. However compelling the arguments in favour of going down the Mote pathway, the authorities need to be convinced! Let's start with a reiteration of some important deliverables. Or to put it another way, some of the most important promises we can make to management:

Ten ways the Mote system will help you transform the way your business uses meetings

1. You can carry out a meeting audit at the outset, and address the issues it throws up. Also a skills audit of your key peoples' meeting performance, as judged by their bosses, their direct reports and peers.

2. You will need fewer meetings overall, and there will

be fewer attendees in Motes compared to traditional meetings.

3. Also the average Mote will be of shorter duration than the average meeting.

4. Decision making will be faster in Motes.

5. Also superior project management, opportunity identification and problem-solving.

6. More work will be done by people who would otherwise have been in meetings.

7. Office culture will change from being dominated by endless meetings.

8. There will be an emergence of the Dynamic Duo / Power of Two spirit.

9. Experts and specialists will be called into Motes as required, and used to best effect, but they will then be released once they have made their contributions and be available for other challenges.

10. People should be much more motivated. They will be working in teams, not individually. Motes will be much more productive and successful. It will be far more fun, as Motes are enjoyable and *new!*

Now let's look wider...

Get the best out of your best people

Let's start with the motivation of having more meeting-free quality time to spend on real work, and also on family and leisure. But in Motes, as opposed to meetings, they will have the chance to work on exciting projects, with their most able colleagues and in the most dynamic format. In the Mote system, they will be developing the differentiated skill of thinking together. Working together is the traditional way of harnessing talents to deliver against goals. THINKING together expands the talent store, and enhances the effectiveness of the subsequent working together stage.

Enhance recruitment

Mote is an innovation. It works better. It helps people work together better. Success beckons for the early adopters. There is a remarkable opportunity for graduates and young hires to learn to become Navigators and meeting professionals. The lexicography helps too. Mote is a brand, authenticated by new language.

Motivate existing staffers

Mote is a development that makes the organisation a better, more progressive place to work, not least as one of the new breed of meeting specialists. The Spirit of Mote is also dedicated to killing the false god of crazy-busyness. Few ambitious organisations take any active steps to prevent their people burning out.

The principles of Mote are appealingly different from win at all costs

Not everyone in the organisation is going to be an idealist – but hopefully some are. Mote offers a very different set of values, and gives permission for empathic attitudes and behaviour way beyond the meeting room.

Orchestrated meetings are far more likely to deliver results

Experience of Mote will convince at least some of the sceptics that managed meetings are far more likely to be successful than the conventional laissez-faire approach. This evidence of the efficacy of Moting will reassure enthusiasts, win over the waverers, and hopefully isolate the nay-sayers.

Mote is strong on soft values, but it also provides an alternative set of criteria for managing that most awkward part of the workforce – successful and cynical senior managers

The meeting audit, and especially the meeting skills assessment, is bound to show that some of the worst meeting behaviour comes from some of the most senior members of the community. A commitment by the company to Mote will require these powerful executives to reorient and change attitudes and behaviour if they are going to become regular Leaders and Moters.

The Mote revolution means a change from looking at meetings as one-offs to seeing Motes as campaigns

This will do more than just change expectations. The logistics of setting up, say, the conventional stakeholder meeting, are such that it is apparently acceptable to delay a critical meeting until one or more key colleagues are back from Germany, or vacation, or illness. So, nothing can happen for three weeks. Then we have an unproductive, inconclusive gathering. And it is going to take two weeks to reconvene! If we are planning a campaign of Motes to deliver the positive change within perhaps eight weeks, the logistics and facilitation are wholly different.

Let's start with small numbers – and keep it that way

A Mote series will start with more than one person. The process is after all as dedicated to discouraging dictatorship as much as it is to avoiding faux democracy. But it will start with far fewer people than a lot. Leader and Navigator will probably be tasked with launching the Mote series or campaign. Stepladder will at the same time cast carefully and ensure that there is no snowball effect. Once everyone sees how well small agile teams work, there will be little enthusiasm for going back.

Mote's effect will not be confined to company HQ

As soon as an organisation starts to feel the benefit of Mote, it will want to extend the system to encounters with outsiders – sister companies, international affiliates, customers, clients, suppliers, partners. The principles and Spirit of Mote will already have spread within the organisation to meetings other than strategic and dynamic sessions. Assembly, Briefing, Team, Learning and Selling meetings will all benefit from a dose of empathy and an outbreak of better behaviour.

Some soundbites to convince the doubters!

- Meetings are often stationary coaches with many people on board, whereas a Mote should be a streamlined

vehicle seating as few people as possible.
- With a Mote you simply have to leave egos and adversarial behaviour outside the door.
- Motes are not just better meetings. The Mote system also makes individuals and organisations function faster and more efficiently.
- Motes are the meetings clever people want to go to, because they are where transformations happen better, quicker and with fewer moving parts.
- Creativity and innovation CAN happen in a Mote.
- Great Moters are not defined by their titles, but by how they perform as a team.

Hard evidence from auditing existing meeting practice – a real life example – Summary findings from the Geometry Global survey

An extensive company-wide survey on meetings and meeting culture was distributed at Geometry Global, a leading international brand activation agency. Employees at all levels and across departments took part and answered questions on everything from why do you have meetings to what is the most effective form of meeting. The entire survey and its results can be accessed and perused on the Mote website – *http://motemeeting.com*

What follows are the most pertinent findings and answers from this revealing survey:

Meeting Booking system

- We need a booking system that works.
- We should implement a simple booking system that works so that each meeting can take place in a meeting room (lot of time is wasted running round the building trying to find a meeting room).

Prioritising meetings, and avoiding 'Ambush' meetings

- The amount of 'ambush' style meetings that take place are overwhelming – these are meetings that either have no calendar invite or are booked less than an hour before the meeting is due to take place.
- Sometimes there is no getting around a quick catch-up meeting, but when you are doing this two, three, four times a day it becomes very hard to manage your time and get work done.
- Regular, planned meetings need to be prioritised and booked selectively, to obviate the need for disruptive instant meetings.

Inviting the right people

- If it is a decision making meeting, only invite people that can make decisions.
- Invite only those who are actually needed – others can be made aware in follow-up meetings or through meeting notes distributed afterwards.
- Have the right people in the room. Too many people are there just to state their negative opinion.
- Mandatory acceptance or decline of invitations.

- When pitching, smaller committed teams.
- Have a moderator to guide the meeting and make sure it doesn't go off topic.

Objectives

- 'At an agency I used to work at, every single meeting was started with the phrase, 'The purpose of this meeting is….'. It seemed like a silly exercise at first, but as time went on it was an invaluable trick to set the tone every time you met as a group'.
- Have a clear objective and agenda for the meeting.
- Planning ahead and have a clear objective.
- Outline clear objectives at the beginning of the meeting. Ensure those objectives are met. Ensure the right people are in the room to meet those objectives.

Agenda

- Agenda or Synopsis within meeting invite to ensure people know what the meeting is about.
- Agree agenda upfront.
- Clear agenda and plan of action to get things done.
- Have appropriate and approved documentation to supplement or run the meeting.

Timekeeping

- Make it a mandatory habit to arrive on time for a meeting.
- Make sure that time slots are indicated for each agenda item and that these are adhered to.

- Attendee punctuality: there is a counter-productive tendency for people to be quite lackadaisical about time.
- Have people show up on time.
- Late starts to meeting are frustrating for everyone and mean that the objectives cannot be achieved.
- BE ON TIME! Ensure our attendance is needed and relevant.
- Biggest bugbear for me is people arriving late for meetings.
- Meeting etiquette to be set and people reminded, including timekeeping.
- Avoiding last minute changes to meeting times.
- Previous meetings in the booked room finishing on time.

Comments about the meeting environment

- The environment for client meetings is not good.
- Meeting rooms not inspiring enough.
- Environment is a huge factor. Meetings in 3c (comfy, relaxed sofas) almost always end up with clearer outcomes and points of action, compared to meetings in 3a (cold, stark, not very collaborative).
- Meeting rooms should be far more inspirational for people. It would be good to have more break-out areas.
- More creative looking meeting rooms to help creative thinking.
- Environments are cold and sterile and do not encourage brainstorming sessions to flow.

- Better environment – often too crowded / noisy /close to other meetings.
- Not enough break-out areas to have informal meetings.
- More whiteboards.

Sticking to the agenda

- Training on meeting management will certainly help to stay on track at meetings.
- A lot of the meetings I attend are great and productive, but some can get wildly off subject, and ultimately you leave not knowing what you accomplished.
- Ensure that everyone sticks to the agenda and doesn't wander off topic.

Minutes

- Someone should take notes and send out a little list of things as a conclusion after every meeting.
- Keep them short. Circulate notes/call reports afterwards.
- Very quick and brief minutes (bullet points/actions) so that only those directly necessary have to attend, and everyone else could be brought up to speed.

What can we learn from an audit?

Meeting audits are very revealing. It is one thing to suggest improved process and best practice, but what matters is the degree of progress required, compared with what is happening now on a day to day basis. It can be seen clearly from the above report that people become frustrated at minor but continuous breaches of common sense and meeting etiquette.

Introducing Mote is likely to be much more effective having established through an audit where frustration lies. It makes sense to set out clear goals and performance targets for Mote.

Extending the audit to a capability assessment of key players

Very few organisations regard individual meeting performance as a differentiated skill. But it undoubtedly deserves it. An expert assessment of the meeting participation and contribution skills of managers and executives would provide valuable inputs to the adoption of the Mote system. Assessing meeting performance and ability is going to be far more effective if it is done on the '360 principle' - it can be awkward to sell in, but it is the best way. There are HR implications in terms of the wisdom of recruiting pathfinders not mavericks, the constructive use of graduates and interns, and the development of professional meeting specialists. Almost certainly this would also lead to the systematic use of profiling in team building, and coaching on the way executives operate, work, and contribute to company goals, as well as retraining to reduce or eliminate poor meeting behaviour and etiquette.

The ten most likely dividends from investing in Mote

1. Highly defined decision making culture
2. Opportunities defined better, so that they can be realised more quickly
3. Problems solved better and faster
4. Meetings that aren't run on Mote lines become less attractive and more frustrating
5. Culture becomes more focused on work/life balance – less on sitting in meetings
6. Rise of the Mote specialist, which will have a beneficial effect on *all* meetings
7. Greater efficiency overall
8. Higher individual and collective productivity as projects move faster and more successfully
9. Enhanced growth and profitability
10. Morale, satisfaction and loyalty all grow

Use Mote to start Moteing

So how do we start? Quite simply by using Mote!

In 1964 Canadian sage Marshall McLuhan coined the phrase 'The Medium is the Message'. His million-seller book would also have carried that title had a typesetter not made a prescient error and set 'The Medium is the Massage' instead. McLuhan was apparently alluding to the unintended consequences of change, and indeed he first defined the thought as follows, 'this is merely to say that the personal and social consequences of any medium – that is, of any extension of ourselves – result from the new scale that is introduced into our affairs by each extension of ourselves, or by any new technology.'

However his famous phrase is more usually used to refer to the influence of context over content. So I can suggest to you that if you are impressed by the idea of Mote, and want to try it out in your company, pick a Leader and a Navigator, and give them the challenge of assembling a team of Moters to start the process. Here is how a Mote process can get under way, proving that McLuhan's 'Medium is the Message' is still a live concept.

1. Alex Lubar, Global CMO McCann Worldgroup, based at McCann in New York, was impressed with the idea of Mote and the benefits it could bring. He thought it would be a good idea to try it out with teams at McCann New York.

2. CEO Chris Macdonald agreed to a trial, and Alex is the designated Leader of the project.

3. Alex chooses Mike Tsang as Navigator. A working lunch extends into a fairly lengthy meeting. At the end of this session Alex and Mike are supercharged with enthusiasm for trialling Mote in three different applications:

   a. The Mote project itself – as an example of a change management innovation.

   b. New Business – the principal engine of agency growth.

   c. Account Management on a big account – an

opportunity to develop a more productive system for managing the day to day client relationship, and in particular creative development.

4. Mike invites A and B to join Alex and himself at the first Mote early in January. A is a planner, B a HR specialist.

5. The Motion is pretty simple: how can we get Mote off the ground as fast as possible, and is it best to start with just one application, or run all three in parallel?

6. Leader and Navigator meet ahead of the Mote to pre-plan the first session and also to agree an outline critical path and schedule, with a view to completing the initial part of the trial by end-March. They agree that there is little to be gained by debating the merits of Mote in this first session. After all, management have already agreed in principle. Far more constructive to provide A and B with a concise guide to the principle, philosophy and practice of Mote as a pre-read. That will save unnecessary time answering questions.

7. As Leader, Alex wants to get the Mote off to a flying start. He spends the first ten minutes on a joint presentation with Mike fast-forwarding to the five most powerful potential long-term benefits of using the Mote system for dynamic meetings:

   a. Faster response to new business opportunities, and improved win rate

   b. Streamlined account handling by bringing clients into the Mote way, better relationships, and greater organic growth

   c. Significant and measurable savings in people hours and cost by having fewer, more productive meetings/ Motes

   d. Considerable people development benefits, as McCann staffers learn a more collaborative way of working together

   e. Enthusiasm spreading from the Mote Squad outwards as early adopters reap the benefits of enhanced job satisfaction and life/work balance

8. He then sets out the project goal – torture-testing the Mote system as an accelerator of transformations, and as a superior environment for developing collaborative and productive working together.

9. In the discussion that follows A explores practical aspects of adapting agency modus operandi in both new and client business and B talks about the HR implications. Agreement that it does make sense to push ahead with all three applications.

10. Mike the Navigator and resource investigator is tasked with planning follow-up sessions and the specialists and stakeholders who will need to be involved.

Alex Lubar sums up the success of the trial thus, 'For an industry that is driven by the need for swift, collaborative and informed decision-making, Mote gave us an opportunity to bring the brightest and the best to the table at exactly the right time for maximum impact. We still have some way to go in terms of Mote implementation but the initial signs are that we are going to see a significant rise in decision-making effectiveness.'

Recommended sequence of events for getting Mote off the ground

1. Decision at Board level to tackle meeting problems seriously.

2. Invite Mote expert to present the case for introducing the Mote System and the Spirit of Mote and advise on implementation.

3. Sharing with managers and staff why this project could be a pathway to transforming the way people in the company work together, manage change, drive projects and make decisions.

4. Acceptance that the company's process and culture may require an overhaul, as well as the meeting regime.

5. Commence a Mote sequence to consider the optimum way of doing this. Maybe on the 'Need it. Get it. Do it. Live it' principle, mixing formal learning, coaching and feedback on the job. Set timelines.

6. Audit existing meeting practice
   a. Classify the different kinds of meeting currently in use
   b. Objectives and goals of these meetings. Long term? Short term? (Sometimes better mid-term)
   c. How many meetings – a week, a day?
   d. Back-to-backs? How often? All the time?

e. Who organises?

f. Are meetings planned properly? Or is it simply a question of booking a room and sending out invites?

g. Who is involved in the organisation?

h. How many attendees, and what roles do they perform?

i. Any sense that meetings are team affairs? Or are 'democracy' and assembling stakeholders the prime drivers?

j. Innovative or unusual venues or formats?

k. How long do the meetings last?

l. What do they achieve?

m. What do they cost in both money and time?

n. Collateral cost?

o. Benefit/cost analysis

p. Other options?

q. How are behaviour and etiquette? What about the obvious meeting traps?

r. Benchmark these finding against norms

7. Survey and interview individual managers and executives

a. Their views

b. Their skills

c. Benchmarked assessment of those views and skills

8. Analyse gap between current performance and optimum – and calculate work needed to raise standards.

9. Coach both System and Spirit of Mote

a. Five Principles of Mote:
   i. GAME PLAN
   ii. SMALL AGILE TEAM
   iii. STEPLADDER
   iv. PERFORMANCE
   v. SPIRIT
b. Managed and orchestrated meetings
c. Team meetings – thinking together and working together. A Mote isn't a meeting, so much as a team in action
d. Role of Leader (to partner in order to bring about and manage change)
e. Role of Navigator (to become a career meeting professional, facilitator, resource investigator and receiver and transmitter of inbound and outbound info
f. Role of Moters
g. Role and usage of remoters
h. Setting Motions
i. Decision making technique
j. Spirit of Mote – empathic behaviour and meeting etiquette (avoiding obvious meeting traps)
k. Skills required
l. Prioritisation – promoting thinking, creativity and focus, and tackling selfishness, 'crazy busyness', multi-tasking, poor etiquette and behaviour
m. Extension of Spirit of Mote to other meetings and the workplace in general

10. Train teams and individuals on how Mote works, and on behaviour, etiquette, empathy and agreeableness.

11. Train individuals on profiling and balancing teams.

12. Plan regular reviews to ensure progress is maintained.

13. Best information in and out:
    - Technology
    - No need to use meetings to catch up
    - Reduce Fear Of Missing Out among people who will now not be participating in meetings to which they are normally invited
    - Insist on pre-reads and post-meeting action summaries being read

Key questions about introducing Mote

A. How relevant is Mote in an era of handheld devices and always-on data and info?

There has never been a time when it is so vital to update and upgrade interpersonal and interactive meeting techniques. It makes sense to use people thinking and working together for what only PEOPLE can do. Many of us travel a lot by air. Just visualise an aircraft or a lounge full of all the devices taken on board by a plane-load of people. These travellers are incredibly connected. They are constantly in touch with colleagues, customers and client, as well as with partners, family and friends. Paradoxically they are able to make far more progress in the air and on the road than they would be in the office. Because in the office, there is a good chance they would be in meetings, only able to make sporadic contact with the outside world. But if they are tasked with driving strategic projects, they do need to meet colleagues in a dynamic meeting format like Mote.

B. Should we try to turn all meetings into Motes?

No that does not make sense at all. Mote was designed primarily for **Dynamic and Strategic Meetings** – which are meetings with a purpose: eg creating and managing change, driving projects, working towards a significant decision.

Not all meetings are like that. **Assembly Meetings** (see Chapter 2 for these definitions) are meetings that are more or less obligatory for people who have been elected to committees, boards, councils, parliaments and so forth. The role of attendees is prescribed. There is no justification for restricting discussion and debate, when participants are there to represent the interests of those who have elected them. Big meetings are inevitable, and so are long sessions. You cannot do anything about it.

Briefing Meetings are specifically to tell a group of people what is required of them. There are obvious economies in having all key players in the room at the same time. It's not one way traffic. The prime requirement is for whoever is responsible for delivering the briefing to do so. But it is also important for the recipients of the briefing to be able to ask questions. Briefing meetings can also be meetings to allow management to make announcements and share news and information. It is obviously better, if possible, for people to receive briefs and hear information live. Even a quick meeting is preferable to a few words in an email or on a notice board. Again, there is no problem with numbers.

Team Meetings are often effectively progress meetings for project teams. They are useful for management, and motivating for team members. They tend to be of short duration, and no useful purpose would be served by restricting attendance.

It is difficult to see how **Learning Meetings** could be run on Mote lines, or indeed why you would want to do so. The purpose of this type of meeting is to enable teachers to teach and students to learn, and this applies equally to religious observance.

On the other hand **Selling Meetings**, I believe, could work well with aspects of Mote, whether they consist of one organisation or individual selling to another, or of 'selling up' meetings within companies. Experience of orchestrating meetings between clients and agencies at AAI for over a quarter of a century has convinced me that both the team aspect and the mutual understanding of goals make such meetings more productive. Additionally smaller meetings and shorter sessions (using Mote) tend to work better.

C. What are the features of Mote that will work in other kinds of meeting as well?

First, keeping meetings as lean as possible. When I set out on my road to Mote, I instinctively distrusted the idea of big meetings, largely because so often the bigger the meeting, the slower the progress. A friend told me that his experience is that big meetings tend to produce small decisions, and vice versa. I think that one of the most dangerous sentences in the English language is, 'Let's get all the stakeholders around a table'! That means more people, less airtime per participant, more frustration, and more resistance to change, because stakeholders are, sadly, wedded to keeping things roughly as they are. Also, big meetings are a theatre in which destructive behaviour flourishes.

Secondly, encouraging empathy. Trying to understand the views of others, even if you do not agree with them, is a major lubricant in the meeting room. Good manners, a collaborative attitude, and collegiate and considerate behaviour are the Spirit of Mote. It may be relatively unfashionable as a philosophy, but it has a lot going for it, not just in Motes but in all meetings.

D. What is the most valuable dividend from doing a meeting survey and skills audit?

Almost certainly the dispassionate way it starts the debate within the organisation. Meeting strategy and meeting systems are not familiar subjects on the corporate agenda. 'Meetings happen'. Indeed meetings happen all the time, and considering the massive number of hours in a year given over to debate, there is very seldom any significant time spent debating how an organisation should run its meetings. Agreeing the questionnaire for a Meeting System Survey is a useful exercise in itself. Requiring colleagues to respond is very important. Analysing and interpreting the results tells us a great deal about how we do things, and indeed the extent to which that way may be far from ideal. The reporting back process, sharing the results with colleagues, is the beginning of the process of putting things right.

E. Once you have analysed results from a meeting survey, what is the next step?

The obvious (indeed the conventional) answer is that the findings should be discussed at length across the organisation. But that it is so out of keeping with Mote!

I would suggest that the next step should be to try new and different things, new and different meeting systems and process. The meeting problem is so serious that attitudinal change is wholly inadequate. To make any difference people have to behave differently. Mote has several advantages in that regard:

- Leaders are far more effective than chairmen
- Navigators offer an organisational and directional dynamic totally lacking in the average 'free-flow' meeting
- Stepladder delivers fewer and more appropriate Moters and Remoters, when you want them, and lets them go when you don't – so the room will contain a lean, agile team, not a departure lounge of individuals
- Empathy beats the hell out of the law of the jungle

These four characteristics will show how smaller, shorter

sessions are so much more effective than big, traditional meetings. Try it out and then discuss the difference.

F. Where is resistance to adopting Mote most likely to come from and what is the best way to deal with it?

Obviously this is going to differ from one company to another, but let me offer five possible candidates:

- Poor decision makers
- People who tend to be resistant to change
- People who have spent so much time in meetings over the years that they are probably no more productive outside the conference room than they are in it
- Those who congenitally or persistently behave badly in meetings
- People who are worried about missing out (FOMO), and specifically concerned that their influence will diminish if they are not invited to at least three meetings a day.

What can be done about this? We have agreed that introducing Mote requires a change in philosophy, a change in organisation, a change in process and, importantly, a change in people. Some of the change in people (to deal with the problems identified above) can be coached and trained. In other respects only different people, committed and trained in the Mote way, will deliver the full benefit of Mote. There is no easy answer to dealing with the five candidates. I am sure that large numbers of business people embrace the general principle of fewer, smaller, quicker meetings. Once they see that Motes not only have these distinctive characteristics, but also deliver greater efficiency and productivity, they will become supporters.

I truly believe that empathy and the Spirit of Mote will make a big difference. People will come to understand that Mote makes meetings pleasanter and more fun – because of better behaviour and a warmer atmosphere. When they also associate Motes with more productivity and better outcomes, a lot of resistance will disappear.

FOMO is hard to deal with, simply because lack of confidence and fear are such strong motivators. Clearly management (and it is a management responsibility) will have to ensure that everybody of talent, responsibility and ambition have the opportunity to become Moters. Missing out on all key meetings is clearly demotivating. Hopefully people will come to understand that attending fewer, better Motes, and having more time to work and live their lives is a good trade.

◆ MOTEBITE

Mote will transform not just the way your company does meetings. It will change the way your company does almost everything

Make time for 'Gurumax'!

I have been struck during my research on meetings and the potential for Mote by what I can only describe as a widespread disinclination to learn new tricks. Worryingly this tendency seems to be more pronounced the steeper one climbs the organisation.

It doesn't seem that many years ago when it was in vogue for corporations to be seen as learning organisations. A classic example was ICI, chaired by the flamboyant John Harvey-Jones between 1982 and 1987. At that time it was one of the biggest and most important British companies. After Harvey-Jones it was redirected into becoming a performance organisation, with disastrous consequences.

Researching a book ensures frequent trips up numerous learning curves, and very pleasurable it is. As a result I have become a passionate advocate of what I have termed 'Gurumax' – the movement to instil a learning culture and an appetite for innovation and new skills. 'Gurumax' signifies identifying as many relevant Gurus as possible, engaging with them, and using their expertise and knowledge to the maximum. In this way we can encourage experts to reach out even further into not just the organisations that habitually value coaching, training and expertise, but also what we might call guru deserts.

I just feel we don't learn enough. We are too self-reliant. We are too confident in the validity of our experience. Most of us regard our education as over. There are so many clever experts, professors, gurus. Most of the learning is freely accessible – the only cost is facilitating and organising the process.

The 'Gurumax' philosophy is that it is important that we all maintain a commitment to continuous learning, and that we share good thinking and good ideas. There is no point in people publishing books and our having them on our shelves unless they are read and used. Equally, we should take advantage of the blogosphere to learn and pass on wisdom.

A little discussed collateral problem with the meetings that cram the diaries of crazy-busy executives is that it leads to clever people running on empty, relying on a mixture of instinct, old knowledge and company culture and practice. My hope is that Mote will attract their attention, and stimulate them to be not just aware of the meeting minefield, but enthusiasts for using innovatory solutions, and coming up with others.

'Gurumax' could encourage and cajole actual and potential Moters to take time out to learn from the very brightest and best contemporary thinkers, instead of spending every week, month, year relying on old knowledge. Evidently the world divides quite sharply into people who buy and read business books, people who buy them but don't tend to read them, and those who neither buy nor read them! With a plethora of ways of disseminating thinking and ideas open to us, there are many possibilities, and it will make people development and training much easier if HR can call on a regular stream of expert stimulus.

◆ MOTEBITE

We don't learn enough. We are too self-reliant. We are too confident in the validity of our experience. Most of us regard our education as over. Mote is the opportunity to learn and innovate.

"So how did the meeting go?"

Chapter 12

THE SECRETS OF BEING A GREAT MOTER – AND A STAR PERFORMER -AT EVERY MEETING YOU ATTEND

You can learn a business skill that will turbocharge your career prospects. Now you can look forward to meetings with confidence and enthusiasm. And meetings will look forward to having you. This book has focused primarily on the company perspective – and in particular why meetings are wasteful and unproductive. Most of the ideas and recommendations I have put forward are suggestions for companies to take a radical look at the way everyone meets together and works together.

But why would you find Mote an attractive proposition unless it gives you the chance to excel? Turning meetings into a team game won't work unless team members upskill and know what to do. If you are keen to join in the Mote revolution and play your part in dramatically more effective meetings, please read on.

Becoming a much better meeting performer in 20 easy steps

Let's start with the obvious skills and move outwards to

some qualities which are subtler and maybe harder to acquire or develop.

SKILLS

1. Profiling – understanding what makes us all tick

A firm recommendation is to take personality profiling seriously so as to understand oneself better, and your colleagues in enough depth at least to be able to suggest who might form the most effective partners and teams. There's a fairly obvious upside in doing this. But there is a drawback as well. The more you drill down into your own personality, the clearer it will become what you are capable of, and also what you are not suited for. There is no human yet born capable of ticking all the boxes! You will have to choose strong suits, dismiss the ones where you are bound to struggle, and have colleagues lined up to fill the gaps and complement you.

2. Team playing

This chapter is primarily about recognising and honing individual skills, but most of the greatest performers in fields like sport and entertainment are seen at their best in team situations. By their very nature, meetings are collective, but the tradition has not been for team performance. Mote is the exception to that rule. Leader, Navigator and Moters comprise a small team that have to collaborate to be effective. Harnessing the individual skills below is important for personal success, but without behaving synergistically much of the extra performance will be wasted. A good example is that Navigators have to be team players to do their jobs.

3. Presenting and making your case

It is difficult to get far in meetings without being competent at both preparing and delivering presentations. There is plentiful training available in organising material, putting it on MS Powerpoint or some other proprietary presentation software, and performing. It is like serving at tennis and driving at golf. There is more to the sport than getting the ball in play. But it helps enormously. 'Death by Powerpoint' is an exaggeration. All the psychological evidence says that speaker support and visual aids help comprehension, and particularly retention. Nonetheless, very few meetings, let alone Motes, can survive wall-to-wall presentations. We need interaction as well.

4. Conversation / Talking

If presentation is like serving or driving, conversation and articulateness allow us to play the rallies and build a score. There are some really good tips in Alan H Palmer's book *Talk Lean*. He is completely on message with the Spirit of Mote in saying that to win friends and influence people you need to be polite and respectful, and to be very clear in what you say. He advises concentrating on the similarities between people and not the differences. Palmer suggests that meeting participants pay attention to the subtleties of language. Most people aren't empathic, and can sometimes say the right things in the wrong way. Then there's the balance between what's said and unsaid. Unfortunately people can be adversely affected by things that have NOT been said, as well as by things that have been said in the wrong way. Developing conversational skills for meetings is essential for the ambitious Moter. It is the defining skill, and has to be used in different contexts; for instance speaking when presenting or building a case, as already mentioned above. Then there is speaking when responding – more of a reactive skill, but vital nonetheless. Finally the Moter has to be eloquent towards the end of the process when suggesting or supporting solutions.

5. Debating / Arguing a point

Debating is conversation with attitude. There is a fine line between debate and argument. Unfortunately the ubiquity of arguing and interruption on TV and radio has made aggression part of the default setting for debate, which is most unfortunate. Prime Minister's Questions is a particularly bad example. Debating in a non-aggressive, constructive style is a mandatory skill in a Mote. Empathy doesn't mean everyone has to agree about everything all the time!

6. Listening

Listening is the most underrated meeting skill. I was once on an awards jury with five other dominant over-talking alpha males. What a nightmare! You couldn't listen, because everyone was talking at the same time. Listening is difficult; our emotions distort what is actually said and we're busy analysing and formulating responses while the other person is talking. Note-taking can help us to concentrate. Then there is bad listening, where we only hear what we want to hear.

7. Asking questions

The ability to ask good questions – not least 'and what do *you* think?' – is a fundamental skill in any meeting. In a Mote asking questions is really important, because of the vital contribution of the experts and specialists who join as Moters. In order to make a contribution, they need to understand fully what is going on – goals, challenges, problems, difficulties. Equally Leader, Navigator and everyone else also require question and answer sessions to derive maximum benefit from the involvement of the experts.

8. Negotiating / Diplomacy

Empathy is useful in any kind of negotiation. By definition negotiation doesn't work if you try to win on all fronts. You have to prioritise, and establish where you are not prepared to concede and back down, and on what points you will give ground if necessary. The classic definition of empathy – standing in the other person's shoes – sums up the core skill of the negotiator and seeing where your counterpart is coming from. Diplomacy is a related skill to negotiation.

9. Strategist / Tactician / Chess player / Bridge player

Sport, the performing arts, and even the fusion of

entertainment and nourishment that we call a restaurant, have spawned specialist journalists, commentators and pundits. Oddly, meetings haven't. This means that the players have to double up as doers and talkers about it. As an orchestrated and managed meeting format, the Mote demands both strategy in preparation and hands on strategy and tactics in real time once Moting has commenced. Any of the above specialist skills could help prepare a Moter for the challenges of the game.

10. Forecaster

People with predictive ability – whether it comes from applying silence or gut feel – make valuable Moters. It is not given to us for the most part to know what is going to happen, but it helps enormously to be able to make intelligent guesstimates.

QUALITIES

11. Empathy

Empathy makes the biggest single difference between a Mote and an ordinary meeting. So, unsurprisingly, Moters with a natural tendency to being empathic are like gold dust. We can all (and must) try to put ourselves in the shoes of others, but those to whom it comes naturally have a big future in the world of Mote. For many of these altruistic and generous people, Mote makes a welcome change after years of dog eat dog, and a culture of adversarial behaviour.

12. Thick skin

The road to empathy, for those to whom it does not necessarily come naturally, can turn out to be paved with a lack of other people's good intentions. Progress towards creating a genuinely collaborative atmosphere can take time, and during that time a thick skin is a distinct asset...

13. Patience

...as indeed is patience – another prized virtue in a Mote. Each session might be relatively brief, but the series or campaign of Motes is likely to be spread over a reasonable length of time. So being patient -especially as Leader or Navigator – is an important quality.

14. Wisdom

It could be argued that wisdom and empathy are contingent and related qualities. One probably has to be wise to be empathic, and empathic to recognise and practise wisdom. I also believe, perhaps not surprisingly, that age helps make us a bit wiser.

15. Being a good mixer / Charm

Trying to take business skills and attitudes into private and family life can be challenging and unrewarding! It is good to find an opportunity to do the opposite and find a profitable outlet for charm and the ability to mix easily with a variety of people. Any meeting, whether it is a traditional conference, a business or private dinner, or a Mote requires a little ice-breaking and reaching out.

16. Leadership

Mote will only work in an organisation if there is a plentiful supply of determined leaders, whose natural inclination is to drive rather than follow, and lead in preference to chairing. For small, focused Mote sessions, Leaders and traditional leadership skills are essential.

17. Persuasiveness

This is the quality that converts articulateness into making a difference. Persuasiveness tends to be a cocktail of several of the skills above – notably presenting, articulation, debating and negotiation. Oh yes, and charm helps too!

18. Optimism

Good meeting technique requires elements of both glass half-full and half-empty. Far more decisions have gone disastrously wrong through rashness and over-optimism, than because of caution and pessimism. But in the dynamic environment of a Mote, controlled optimism is a distinct asset. The principal reason? Optimism is infectious and motivating, while pessimism is depressing and corrosive. The Spirit of Mote calls for motivation (to coin a phrase!).

19. Sense of history

I have emphasised the 'managed' and 'orchestrated' aspect of the Mote. But even a well-navigated and well-led Mote is capable of twists and turns away from what passes as a script. Being a classy Moter requires the sensitivity to react to new developments and unpredictable situations with a cool and analytical mind. History can be useful here. There aren't many meeting moments that one is seeing for the very first time. Maybe this is another aspect of wisdom.

20. Summing up / Memory

Every Mote, like every other meeting, is destined to end up as a set of minutes. But that doesn't mean one can afford to wait till the end of the Mote to start summing up. Both Leader and Navigator will find their roles enhanced by the valuable quality of being able to summarise the 'story so far', and use this progressive analysis to move everyone forward to the successful resolution of a good Mote or meeting.

How can we define a 'good Mote'?

Think disciplined and tight team – not departure lounge. We have all witnessed the departure lounge scenario, a large room where disparate individuals arrive one by one or two by two. It generally takes the first twenty minutes to make sure everyone who is coming has arrived, and for them to be introduced to each other.

From that unpromising beginning any kind of performance is impossible. The best anyone can hope for is a cross between a team meeting and a briefing meeting. Individuals can be brought up to speed, made aware of whom they will be working with, and given an indication of objectives and time frame. To make any progress we need a Mote.

First and foremost great meetings stem from having the right people there, not people who are surplus to requirements, or picked for who and what they are rather than for what they might be able to contribute. In that way we can assemble the raw material for team building, and align everyone to the achievement of goals, deliverables and outcomes.

Secondly, it is essential not to have too many people overall.

Thirdly, we are not accustomed to seeing meetings as teams. Responsibility has to be shared. You *can* decline to attend. You have far more insight into your schedule and priorities than anyone else. You are paid to think and do, not just blindly obey. If you judge that another commitment should take precedence that is your decision. If you feel that you are not an essential attendee, you should say so. I like the rule of thumb used by Tom Bazeley, UK CEO of M&C Saatchi in London. 'If your presence at a meeting won't make a difference, neither will your absence'.

I don't think there is one simple criterion for a 'good' meeting or Mote. As with most complex entities, there are several elements:

- Well set up
- Right people there
- Clear objectives
- Well run
- Constructive atmosphere
- Good progress
- Good segue into what must happen next

◆ MOTEBITE

Think disciplined and tight team, not departure lounge.

'The right people there'

Meetings are essentially corporate affairs, organised to further the business or purposes of an organisation. But around the table we don't find the Memorandum and Articles of the company, or an organisation chart. We find people, individuals. Not surprisingly the outcome of any meeting, is a function of how well people perform. In a Mote, with a hand-picked team, the focus on those individuals is even more searching.

What will make you a great Moter?

1. Knowing when and how to open and close files

Thinking well is crucial, and thinking ahead of time is how most of us 'open the file', as Tony Crabbe suggests. We all have our pet techniques for this: at a minimum, try opening the file the night before, or in the morning for an afternoon meeting.

2. Paying close attention – listening and body language

Even in a world of compulsive and relentless communicators, it is the skills of listening and observation that separate the leaders from the followers.

3. Taking notes – 'listening with your pen or pencil'

I am an inveterate note-taker and list-maker. I find that writing things down always helps me look ahead, especially in terms of preparing for meetings. Alan Palmer (*Talk Lean*) advocates taking notes on precisely what the speaker is saying, rather than applying an editorial filter. He writes, 'taking notes of what is being said not only gives you richer raw material for constructing a response, but it will actually give you more time to think about your response.'

4. Discipline

We can learn from the findings of the Geometry survey. Timekeeping is crucial to an efficient meeting regime. Nothing annoys dedicated meeting attendees more than meetings that start or end late, and colleagues who fail to turn up on time. Since Motes are effectively team efforts, there are obvious parallels. No one is late for a kick-off or curtain-up, so why is it acceptable to be late for a Mote? Being distracted is an obvious contributor to being late. I feel we have to work very hard to fight external distractions, of which there are so many. People pressure us to take on one more task. We receive invitations that are well meant, but disruptive. Noise is a distraction in so many ways. So is travelling, in virtually any form of transport.

5. Demeanour

The Spirit of Mote shows in attitude and behaviour. For example, smiling helps as an outward and visible sign of friendliness. People prefer to do business with people they like. It is not a complicated concept – and it is testament to how much all decision making is far more influenced by emotion and gut feel than by logic and all those criteria and sub-criteria on which we spend so much time and effort. To be a great Moter it is a big advantage to demonstrate a positive, attractive, likeable demeanour. Not always easy and not always what we feel like doing. It is not always what fits most closely with our personality. It is not even a quality that we can ourselves determine. Demeanour is very much in the eye of the beholder.

6. Not falling into bad Meeting Traps

Let's go back to the 'bad behaviour' and characters identified in chapter 5. Here are some suggestions for addressing some of these problems:

Ego and Domino

Ego is very much a function of personality. Successful individuals with drive often have a strong sense of self. But arrogance is a definite weakness that can inhibit the effectiveness of the team. Domino can be similar in its impact, but tends to be more behavioural than part of the personality profile. A more consciously collaborative and empathic attitude, consistent with the Spirit of Mote, will help a lot. Ego can be restrained, and still a force for good. Domino needs to go. It is not compatible with the style of a Mote.

Adverso

This is a behavioural problem that tends to be environmental, rather than inborn. Any Moter who has bought into Spirit of Mote should be capable of learning to use questioning techniques as an alternative to confrontation. In *Leading with Questions*, Michael Marquardt suggests adopting a style that substitutes asking for telling. Questions can take several forms. For example, a clarification question ('are you saying...?') also stimulates debate, but without being as adversarial as 'I simply don't accept that'. Adverso can – and must be – turned. All that energy should be a force for good.

Interrupto

Interrupting and overtalking are maddening to others, but many Interruptos are blissfully unaware. Waiting until the other person has finished and then asking a question can achieve the same end as interrupting without being alienating. Motes cannot function with bad manners, and interrupting people regularly is unacceptable bad manners.

Defo

Listening is non-negotiable in the world of Mote. Hopefully the more civilised, less frenetic atmosphere of a smaller meeting, without everyone trying to talk at once will help the Defo to participate, switch on, not off, and listen better.

Chato

Chato is prone to side conversations and asides to the detriment of the flow of the meeting. This is probably another bad habit to have arisen directly from big, unproductive meetings. Chato should have no part of a team game like Mote. Everyone in the room will simply be too committed and busy.

Passivo

A passive, non-contributory attitude is unacceptable in a Mote as it entirely lacking in empathy.

Conectado

This familiar figure is connected not to the meeting but to their mobile network or the internet. They always seem to be on one or more screens, texting or emailing. This behaviour cannot be tolerated in a Mote. Frequent breaks are the answer and vital for keeping up concentration and energy levels. And the breaks themselves provide the opportunity to send the email or reply to the call.

Amigo

He or she is so friendly that they can fall into the trap of agreeing with everything – often without being able to say why – and also capable of supporting conflicting positions. Hopefully in the much more structured Mote environment this behaviour will not happen, as it will make a team member look ridiculous.

Absento

The Absento misses the meeting without alerting the Navigator. Given the likely competition for places around the Mote table, this will hopefully not be a problem.

Suppresso and Cosisayso

Unhelpful chair behaviour, either by not allowing people to express their views, or by imposing their own, should not happen in a Mote, given the team nature of the endeavour. The team Leader in a Mote is results orientated, so grandstanding serves no useful purpose.

Wrecko

I described this character above as 'a fully-fledged meeting wrecker. Completely counter-productive. Probably best to exclude from meetings if possible'. Such an individual will never be cast as either Leader or Navigator, and neither will pick a Wrecko as a Moter!
I also identified four 'teacher's pets':

Constructo

Constructive, helpful, well-intentioned. An accomplished and positive debater.

Abierto

Open-minded. Good listener.

Bienvenido

The colleague who is always welcome at any meeting. Easy personality. Charming in a good way.

Perspectivo

Not just stuck in the present. Able to view issues from both a historical perspective, and with an eye to the future.

Each of the last four is going to be welcomed at a Mote with open arms.

Time to Mote!

You know the Mote process, you've learnt the principles, and you've avoided the personal pitfalls for poor meeting etiquette. Before you now confidently engage with Mote, here are a few last minute tips and reminders to help you hit the ground running!

- Mote is designed for strategic, dynamic meetings, and helps to achieve positive change
- Bad meetings waste time and money. People suffer from spending 50%+ of their time in meetings. But people also contribute to meeting problems by behaving badly.
- This bad behaviour stems mainly from meetings being too big (often the result of trying to get all the stakeholders around the table)
- Don't confuse efficiency and democracy!
- Mote is an ancient word for meeting (but still used in Scandinavia), that is repurposed to signify the radical new way of running meetings

- Planned and stage-managed meetings will outperform 'free-flow' sessions
- You need to plan a series of Motes, not just one Mote
- Have a precise Game Plan for focus and to ensure that you meet your goals
- Start small with Leader and Navigator
- Use Stepladder to assemble your focused and agile team
- Think together. Work together. Win together
- Empathy, collaboration and the Spirit of Mote are key
- Smaller, shorter, more collaborative, more productive meetings = a Mote

The future of the meeting is in your hands!

◆ MOTEBITE

We value job titles. We value experience. We value university degrees and business school MBAs. We value skill and technique. But become a great Moter – a true meeting professional – and your potential is unlimited

And now you'll have to excuse me. I have a Mote to go to.

David Wethey, 2015

David Wethey is an author and writer. He has two blogsites **www.makingbetterdecisionsbetter.com** and **http://motemeeting.com** He writes articles and blog posts on decision making, current affairs and advertising for a variety of publications and sites – including a monthly blog for the Marketing Society. Following DECIDE (published Feb 2013 by Kogan Page), his new book is MOTE: The Super Meeting, in which he unveils a revolutionary approach to running meetings.

Born 1944 in Alvechurch Worcestershire, he was educated at St Edward's School Oxford and Jesus College Oxford, where he took an MA in Philosophy Politics and Economics. He is married with four adult children, and lives in Reading Berkshire, and Alderney Channel Islands. He is an avid golfer and watcher of cricket and rugby union. He is a member of the Athenaeum, the RAC, and the MCC.

David's business life has been largely in advertising. He began his career in marketing research with AC Nielsen

Company. He then worked for 20 years in advertising agencies in UK, Continental Europe and Asia. His first agency job was at Pritchard, Wood & Partners the agency where account planning was invented. The agency later became Wasey Quadrant and Wasey Campbell Ewald (at that time #5 in the UK), and David was elected to the Board in 1971. He moved to McCann-Erickson where he was Country Manager in Lisbon and then Kuala Lumpur, and Deputy MD at Harrison McCann London. He was CEO of two major London agencies before establishing his own – Wethey Scott Pocock – in 1980. David left the agency world to start Agency Assessments International (AAI) in 1988.

AAI is headquartered in London, with partners, associates and affiliates around the world. AAI advises large advertisers on appointing communications agencies, building and managing productive partnerships with them, and producing work that is both creative and effective. David has undertaken projects in more than 40 countries. He wrote ISBA's handbook on remuneration and the European Pitch Guide. In 2008 he was awarded an Honorary Fellowship by the IPA for services to the Client/Agency Relationship. He has been a member of the Marketing Society for more than 30 years. He lectures passionately and often on advertising matters.

INSPIRATIONAL WISDOM AND SUGGESTIONS FOR FURTHER READING

Allen, K – *The Hidden Agenda* – Bibliomotion (2012)

Barker, A – *How To Manage Meetings* – Kogan Page (2012)

Belbin, M – *Management Teams: Why They Succeed Or Fail* – Butterworth Heinemann (1981)

Buehler, R, Griffin, D and Ross, M – *The Planning Fallacy: Why People Underestimate Their Task Completion* – Journal of Personality and Social Psychology (1994)

Carnegie, D – *How To Win Friends And Influence People* – Simon and Schuster (1936)

Crabbe, A – *Busy: How To Thrive In A World Of Too Much* – Little Brown (2014)

De Bono, E – *Six Thinking Hats* – Little Brown (1985)

Duhigg, C – *The Power of Habit* – Random House (2012)

Epson/CEBR – *Wasted Time In Meetings: A Survey* – New Statesman (2012)

Fox, E – *Rainy Brain, Sunny Brain* – Heinemann (2012)

Gigerenzer, G – *Gut Feelings: The Intelligence of The Unconscious* – Viking Adult (2007)

Goldsmith, M (with Mark Reiter) – *What Got You Here Won't Get You There: How Successful People Become Even More Successful* – Berrett Koehler (2008)

Gutman, R – *The Hidden Power Of Smiling* – TED (2011)

Harford, T – *Adapt. Why Success Always Starts With Failure* – Abacus (2011)

Kahneman, D – *Thinking Fast And Slow* – Penguin (2011)

Kawasaki, G – *The Top 10 Mistakes of Entrepreneurs* (2013)
http: //www. slideshare. net/GuyKawasaki/top-ten-mistakes-of-entrepreneurs

Kneeland, S – *Effective Problem Solving* – How to Books (1999)

Krznaric, R – *Empathy, A Handbook Of Revolution* – Rider (2014)

Levitin, D – *The Organized Mind* – Viking (2014)

Marquardt, M – *Leading With Questions* – Wiley (2014)

McKeown, G –*Essentialism: The Disciplined Pursuit Of Less* – Crown Business (2014)

Mead, P – *When In Doubt Be Nice* – Silvertail (2014)

MeetingKing. com – *Better, Faster, Fewer Meetings With Less Effort* (2015)

Nutt, P – *Why Decisions Fail* – Berrett Koehler (2002)

Obama, B – *State Of The Union Address* (2015)
https: //www. whitehouse. gov/sotu

Palmer, A – *Talk Lean* – Capstone (2014)

Pearl, D – *Will There Be Donuts?* – Harper Collins (2012)

Peberdy, D and Hammersley, J – *Brilliant Meetings* – FT Prentice Hall (2009)

Pittampalli, A – *Read This Before Our Next Meeting* – Portfolio (2011)

Russo, R and Schoemaker, P – *Decision Traps* – Fireside (1989)

Schulz, K – *Being Wrong* – Harper Collins (2010)

Schwartz, B – *Paradox Of Choice: Why Less Is More* – Harper Perennial (2004)

Segall, K – *Insanely Simple: The Obsession That Drives Apple's Success* – Portfolio Penguin (2012)

Senge, P – *The Fifth Discipline: The Art & Practice Of The Learning Organization (incorporating The Ladder of Influence thinking of Chris Argyris)* – Doubleday (2006)

Solomon, L – *Moments Of Impact: How To Design Strategic Conversations That Accelerate Change* – Simon & Schuster (2014)

Taylor, D – *The Naked Leader* – Bantam (2002)

Thaler, R and Sunstein, C – *Nudge* – Penguin (2009)

Urbane Publications is dedicated to developing new author voices, and publishing fiction and non-fiction that challenges, thrills and fascinates.

From page-turning novels to innovative reference books, our goal is to publish what YOU want to read.

Find out more at
urbanepublications.com